Reconsidering The Apostles' Creed

Professing Contemporary Faith Through Ancient Words

Brand W. Eaton

CSS Publishing Company, Inc.
Lima, Ohio

Reconsidering The Apostles' Creed

FIRST EDITION
Copyright © 2020
by CSS Publishing Co., Inc.

Published by CSS Publishing Company, Inc., Lima, Ohio 45807. All rights reserved. No part of this publication may be reproduced in any manner whatsoever without the prior permission of the publisher, except in the case of brief quotations embodied in critical articles and reviews. Inquiries should be addressed to: CSS Publishing Company, Inc., Permissions Department, 5450 N. Dixie Highway, Lima, Ohio 45807

Library of Congress Cataloging-in-Publication Data:
Names: Eaton, Brand Wesley, author.
Title: Reconsidering The apostles' creed : professing contemporary faith through ancient words / Brand W. Eaton.
Description: First edition. | Lima, Ohio : CSS Publishing Company, Inc., 2020. | Summary: "Provides a brief summary of the historical development of the Apostles' Creed's and contemporary interpretation of each clause of the Creed designed to lead readers into critical reflection on its meaning for living a progressive Christian faith in the world. A more theologically progressive approach is taken in the analyses and interpretations of the clauses of the Creed, while remaining within an orthodox understanding of historic Christianity. The aim of the book is a critical reflection on the Creed that seeks to broaden acceptance of differing doctrinal stances that can be taken while still authentically professing the faith of the Apostles' Creed"-- Provided by publisher.
Identifiers: LCCN 2019046856 | ISBN 9780788029462 (paperback) | ISBN 9780788029479 (ebook)
Subjects: LCSH: Apostles' Creed.
Classification: LCC BT993.3 .E24 2020 | DDC 238/.11--dc23
LC record available at https://lccn.loc.gov/2019046856

For more information about CSS Publishing Company resources, visit our website at www.csspub.com, email us at csr@csspub.com, or call (800) 241-4056.

e-book:
ISBN-13: 978-0-7880-2947-9
ISBN-10: 0-7880-2947-9

ISBN-13: 978-0-7880-2946-2
ISBN-10: 0-7880-2946-0   Digitally Printed

For Reverend Bruce Smay and Reverend Doctor
Jay Wesley House
upon whose shoulders I stand.

Contents

Preface — 7

Introduction — 11
Origins Of The Apostles' Creed

One — 19
I Believe In God, The Father Almighty

Two — 24
Creator Of Heaven And Earth

Three — 28
I Believe In Jesus Christ...

Four — 33
Conceived By The Holy Spirit...

Five — 37
Suffered...Crucified...Buried

Six — 42
The Third Day He Rose From The Dead

Seven — 48
He Ascended Into Heaven...

Eight — 53
He Will Come Again To Judge...

Nine — 58
I Believe In The Holy Spirit

Ten — 62
The Holy Catholic Church

Eleven — 68
The Communion Of Saints

Twelve — 74
The Forgiveness Of Sins

Thirteen — 79
Resurrection And The Life Everlasting

Preface

I never even heard of the Apostles' Creed until I was a teenager. I was dating the girl who eventually became my bride, and going to her church with her was a good way to spend time together. When we said The Apostle's Creed in worship, I had no idea what was going on. Liturgical elements like the words to the creed or the Lord's Prayer weren't included in most worship bulletins in those days. I was too embarrassed to ask what was being said, so I did some research on my own the following week and worked to memorize at least enough of The Apostles' Creed so as not to be embarrassed the next time I came to church with my girlfriend.

It wasn't that I had never been to church before. I was baptized as a child, participated in Sunday school, and worshiped on most Sundays with my family. We just never said the Apostles' Creed in my congregation. In fact, I went through confirmation classes as a young adolescent, professed Jesus Christ as Lord and Savior, and took the vows of membership in The United Methodist Church without ever so much as a passing acquaintance with the Apostles' Creed.

I don't know for sure why this was so, but I have my suspicions. I grew up in a parochial kind of environment in which it was assumed everyone was a Christian of one stripe or another. Catholics, Lutherans, Presbyterians, and Methodists might have their unique nuances, but we all belonged to the same scout troops, the same Lions Club, went to the same school and supported the same PTO. Stating the obvious — belief in God the Father, Jesus the Son, the Holy Spirit, and resurrection — might have been seen as unnecessary, or at least redundant. My congregation was rather "low church," so repeating the same words each week, unless it was the Lord's Prayer, was not seen as particularly edifying.

The children's Sunday school curriculum was built upon a program of biblical literacy and learning Bible stories — Moses and the burning bush, Joshua at Jericho, David and Goliath, Jesus walking on the water, preaching the Sermon on the Mount, feeding the five thousand. I believe that kind of program is pretty commendable. I just don't think it left a lot of room for learning The Apostles' Creed. In fact, I feel pretty confident that some of the Sunday school teachers and leaders felt the Apostles' Creed was non-biblical if not unbiblical. It wasn't in the Old or New Testament; it was printed in the back of the hymnal, and that was a good place for it.

In leading young people through confirmation, I remember my pastor not being concerned with many historic elements of Christianity. His concern was for cultivating in us a personal faith whereby we might be able to profess Jesus as Lord and Savior in front of the congregation with at least a little bit of evangelical integrity. Methodists in those days were still dubious about confirmation classes leading to church membership. John Wesley might have had his Aldersgate experience while hearing read Luther's "Preface to Romans," but most of his spiritual heirs I grew up around seriously doubted if a twelve-year-old could have an authentic conversion experience in the church basement while in religion classes — even if they were led by the pastor.

Today, even in the place where I grew up, the "evangelical consensus" (if there ever was such a thing), is gone. Fifth-generation Protestants and Roman Catholics now share the community with immigrant Muslims, Buddhists of various ethnic backgrounds, Hare Krishnas, and secular atheists. Some of the response by Christian denominations to the growing religious pluralism of today has been to lift up their own particular doctrinal emphases, in order to better define themselves in this pluralistic milieu, in ways that lead to division rather than unity. That response often allows little room for personal reflection by which individual Christians might come to "own" their faith. While it is important for Christians of differing denominations to understand how we differ, it is truly significant for us to be able to state clearly to non-Christians the beliefs we claim to share. It is also important to be able to articulate a heartfelt personal faith — like my confirmation pastor sought to inculcate in us during those times in the church basement. Although I may be a "late comer" to The Apostle's Creed, I believe it is our best starting point in that project.

Having said all of that, honesty requires of me a qualification with regard to what follows. In the essays in this book I have explicated The Apostles' Creed from my own position of personal faith and my experience of a particular Protestant religious tradition. My goal is certainly not that readers adopt them uncritically, as they are written as a vehicle for Christian personal reflection and growth in personal faith. I want to inspire thoughtful reconsideration of The Apostles' Creed as a means that can help adult Christians articulate their faith honestly and genuinely in an increasingly pluralistic religious milieu. Thus, I have included a few questions for further reflection at the end of each chapter to promote that process.

So, in commending what follows to the reader, I would misquote 2 Kings 10:15 and parrot some of John Wesley from his sermon, "Catholic Spirit:"

Is thine heart right, as my heart is with thy heart? If it be, give me thine hand.

The Apostles' Creed

*I believe in God, the Father Almighty,
creator of heaven and earth.*

*I believe in Jesus Christ, his only Son, our Lord
who was conceived by the Holy Spirit,
born of the Virgin Mary,
suffered under Pontius Pilate,
was crucified, died, and was buried;
he descended to the dead.
On the third day he rose again;
He ascended into heaven,
is seated at the right hand of the Father,
and will come again to judge the living
and the dead.*

*I believe in the Holy Spirit,
the holy catholic church,
the communion of saints,
the forgiveness of sins,
the resurrection of the body
and the life everlasting. Amen.*

Introduction

Origins Of The Apostles' Creed

Where do we look for the beginnings of this summary of Christian faith, used in worship as an affirmation of faith and declaration of allegiance to the way of Jesus Christ? Until the fifteenth century, this question was succinctly answered by an ancient and pious legend. According to the legend, the apostles were on the cusp of parting from one another to take up their post-Pentecost commission of making disciples of all nations. However, they believed it necessary to first determine a firm unified content for their preaching so that they should not be found spreading personal opinions for the true teaching of the gospel. Being filled with the Holy Spirit, they sat down together and, through the wisdom each possessed, contributed a clause to the creed. Later, promoters of the legend pointed to their own rather arbitrary division of the creed into what was seen by them as twelve different clauses to support the truth of the legend.

With the coming of the Age of Enlightenment in the eighteenth century, doubts that had been percolating for some years before regarding the reliability of the legend of The Apostles' Creed gave rise to a fuller historical evaluation of the creed's origins. Modern creedal studies were born, and critical historical efforts to gain an understanding of The Apostles' Creed as a development through time eventually displaced the acceptance of the legend. Nevertheless, the church has continued to see the creed as an ancient summation of "the faith which was once delivered unto the saints" (Jude 3, KJV).

Scholars in creedal studies have come to some general outlines of agreement. There do remain some differences among them on what most of us would see as minor points of development. What is shared here is certainly not meant to be a deep, scholarly investigation of the creed's beginnings, or a survey of creedal studies. This brief introduction relies on those general outlines of agreement regarding the origins and development of The Apostles' Creed that modern scholars have reached.

Catechism And Baptismal Professions

Early in history, Christian communities realized the need for a uniform way of teaching the faith to new believers who were candidates for baptism. Each community developed a rudimentary series of questions with responses used in preparing baptismal candidates. "Do you believe in God the Father? Do you believe in Christ Jesus, son of God? Do you believe in the Holy Spirit?" The earliest catechism may have been that simple, and the responses perhaps no more than responding to the question in the affirmative: "Yes, I believe."

While these catechisms and baptismal queries were locally developed, they did not lack some consistency from place to place, as the various communities of faith had contact across the miles — first through the itineracy of the early apostles and later through ecumenical fellowship maintained by the various bishops. As these semi-formal catechisms enjoyed development, additions to the three-question foundation in particular localities came to be shared from place to place. Of course, this raises a question about what led to the development and addition of material.

It is possible that the early baptismal confessions gained sub-clauses and additions as the early church developed a greater level of theological reflection. However, in the earliest years, this kind of endeavor was not much engaged as the church struggled to survive persecutions. As the church grew and gained even a tacit acceptance within the dominant pagan Roman culture, the "breathing room" for theological reflection and development became possible. It is more probable that the expansion of the early semi-formal baptismal confession was made necessary in order to distinguish Christianity from many other salvation cults and mystery religions that had sprung up in late antiquity.

Early Development

The Roman world was rife with belief systems, whose adherents claimed a body of knowledge or insight into secret rituals that could lead to personal enlightenment and immortality. The official Roman cult of the gods was never meant to provide this kind of religious meaning, but had developed from earlier Greek mythology as a way to explain how the world as it was came to be, to give it order, and to provide a foundation for its social and political organization. As far as any personal spiritual life or meaning, people had to look elsewhere — and they did. As different belief systems, cults, and mystery religions came into contact with each other through the cosmopolitan world of the Roman Empire, there came to be a great deal of religious *syncretism*: adopting and adapting and co-opting the rituals or beliefs of one cult or sect by another or others.

Given this context, it would have been an easy thing for early Christianity to have become a mish mash of philosophies and beliefs. Other belief systems did take on Christian ideas and thought, adapting them to their own designs. The person of Jesus was, by some, developed into a sort of half-human avatar who communicated cosmic secrets to his closest followers, which would allow them to escape physical existence, deny suffering, and defy death. Some of these groups were known as *gnostics*, after the Greek word *gnosis*, meaning knowledge. Others, because of their belief in a Jesus who only appeared human, while not really being human, have been called *docetists*, after the Greek word *dokeo*, meaning "to seem" or "to appear."

In order to clearly define and protect the Christian faith from syncretism, one of the strategies was to more fully develop and define what was being confessed through the different clauses in the catechisms used for baptismal instruction and profession. Thus, God the Father came to be more fully confessed as Creator of heaven and earth. This helped to define the Christian God from other ideas that the divine Father of Jesus was different from the God of the Hebrew Bible responsible for the material creation, which some sects saw as inferior and a prison for "spiritual beings."

The clause confessing Jesus as the Messiah, or Christ, came to be much more fully developed, probably first because belief in

Jesus as Savior and Lord was primary to any Christian confession. But, there was also a growing need to make clear that this Jesus who was being confessed "suffered under Pontius Pilate," truly died, and was buried like any real human being. It was necessary to make clear that he was, indeed, born of a human mother who had a name. However, he was defined as human with a divine origin in his conception through a unique work by the Spirit of God.

At least with regard to the fuller development of the first two clauses in what were generally three-part baptismal confessions used by local Christian communities, the need to make finer definitions in the face of potential religious syncretism and co-opting of the gospel message played a major role.

The Roman Creed

As Christianity achieved not only a level of acceptance but actual official establishment as the faith of Rome under Emperor Constantine and his successors, the formalization of catechetical instruction and the transformation of baptismal confessions into declaratory statements of faith began to take place in full measure. Now more than before, theological reflection and doctrinal development began to take place in the Church catholic, along with formal liturgical worship. It can be assumed that the choice of baptismal catechism by the local bishop held sway across whatever variants had previously been used across a particular district. This was particularly true for the Roman church, which was so much under the influence of imperial pomp and circumstance. Consequently, the baptismal questions used at Rome were among the first to take shape as a declaration of faith recited during the worship service.

With the opportunity afforded church leaders for greater theological reflection, the Roman Creed enjoyed further development and refining, particularly with regard to the third major clause and the subsequent sub-clauses: "I believe in the Holy Spirit, the Holy Church, the remission of sins, etc." While the final formal state of the Old Roman Creed is not quite what the western Church has known as The Apostle's Creed for most of the past 1000 years, it is very close in form, and its known history and use provides a great deal of insight into the development of The Apostles' Creed as we have it.

Origins Of The Apostle's Creed

Appearance Of The Apostles' Creed Known Today

The oldest manuscript of the Apostles' Creed as we know it today is found in a missionary manual composed by a Benedictine abbot named Priminius. Historians date the composition of this manual to between AD 710 and 724, probably at the abbey of Reichenau, which Priminius founded under the patronage of Charles Martel, Prince of the Franks. Its form is obviously owing to the Old Roman Creed first known some four hundred years earlier. However, there had been a great deal of creedal development across the church of the Mediterranean world by the eighth century, and the declaration of faith used in worship at Rome in the eighth century had become the Constantinopolitan Creed — known popularly today as the Nicene or Niceno-Constantinopolitan Creed.

It seems that the Old Roman Creed had come to be displaced below the Alps by the Constantinopolitan Creed in all circumstances as the formal statement of faith in the church. However by the sixth century, the Roman provinces north of the Alps had been conquered by German tribes. These people subsequently became of the object of missionary activity, and eventually converted to catholic Christianity. The Old Roman Creed was the basis for instruction in the faith of these groups by Benedictine and other missionaries.

When Charlemagne came to establish his vast Frankish Christian Empire across what is now much of northern Europe, he sought to reestablish formal education and a regularization of liturgical practice in the church in his own domains. The creed that Charlemagne's court decreed to be memorized by the clergy, taught to the faithful, and recited in worship was the Old Roman Creed brought by the missionaries years before, albeit bearing some minor changes it had undergone through the years. In the midst of great ferment and change in northern Europe, the Old Roman Creed had survived and experienced further development as the preferred baptismal confession of the Germanic Church.

As Charlemagne's power came to bear greater influence over the church and Bishop of Rome than the Greek-speaking Byzantine Church centered at Constantinople, the Old Roman Creed, now more fully developed and known as the Creed of the Apostles, made its way back to acceptance officially in the Roman liturgy. After the formal split of the Christian world between Roman and Eastern churches in 1054, the Apostles' Creed as we have it today remained primary for all western Christianity.

The Apostles' Creed And Contemporary Debate

Late twentieth-century scholarship has seen the development of a popular school of thought concerning the history of Christianity based upon a theory that the "Great Church," as the church catholic that gained establishment status is sometimes called, formalized doctrine in a somewhat hostile way in order to create "insiders" and "outsiders" and enhance the power of the clergy. This theory seems to run along the line that the bishops and other clergy were intent on labeling as heretical those they perceived as threats to their position and power. Attached to this is a great deal of suspicion that the clergy of the imperial church were exceedingly misogynistic, manipulative, and controlling. Doctrinal development according to this theory was solely a matter of building a system to preserve and institutionalize the power of the church and its clergy.

Without wanting to write off this entire school of thought, its position in the long study of Christian historical inquiry bears some scrutiny. It cannot be completely denied that leaders of the early institutional church, as in any age, were influenced by both the acquisition of power and the pressure of political power exerted upon them. However, this admission is a long way from seeing every priest and bishop in the church of the Imperial Age acting as a power-hungry despot. Much of that thinking, I believe, is a reading of the abuses of the late-Medieval Roman Church under the thumb of corrupt popes back into the first centuries of the Christian era.

If the development of the Apostles' Creed is seen as the work of a power-grabbing church intent upon casting out certain rivals as heretics, you will have a different take on the origin of the Apostles' Creed than the one outlined in the preceding paragraphs. Controversy over what was, and was not, acceptable to believe had its role in the creed's formation. But it didn't start out as a means to "divide and conquer," and its later development into the creed known today seems to owe as much to its use in Christian formation as did its birth in the baptismal training of

Origins Of The Apostle's Creed

the first Christian converts of the apostolic age.

Having now spent some time looking at how we got the Apostles' Creed, let's turn to reflecting upon how the creed both informs and professes an authentic twenty-first century Christian faith.

One

I Believe In God, The Father Almighty

When I was a boy of about eleven, my friends and I discovered a swimming hole in the Tuscarora Creek. It's not that others had never swum there before; somebody told us about it. We were also told about the eddy at the downstream end of the hole that fed into an underground channel. If you swam into that eddy and got caught by the whirlpool into the underground stream — there wasn't any hope of survival. Asking contemporary Christians to rethink how and what they profess in saying the Apostles' Creed might be a little like swimming into that eddy.

Some of us come from traditions in which creeds are not accepted, and are, in fact, held in suspicion as human deceptions. I remember learning from a clinical pastoral education supervisor about the "personal theologies" we all carry around. If we are serious about our faith, it is personal and we develop a set of personal beliefs that we live by. What we confess from a creed or confession of faith is often something different from what we actually live out in our lives. It could be said that we profess a certain belief with words, but we make our confession by our actions. So some might find the value of a serious reconsideration of the Apostles' Creed rather dubious.

The fact is we live in an increasingly pluralistic religious world. The need to be able to articulate the core of Christian faith in the course of daily interaction with others is not something faced only by a few clergy who participate regularly in interfaith meetings and dialogues. Our personal theologies may remain just that — personal — but our profession as Christians is a public matter, and it is increasingly incumbent upon us if we are going to be responsible to our profession to be able to tell non-Christians about the bedrock of faith upon which our personal theologies find their foundation.

Ironically, how we talk with people of other faiths, and no faith, about the core of the historic Christian faith relies on logic which is deeply personal. Thus, to say, "I believe in God, the Father almighty" is not the same as saying, "I believe that there is a God." To say, "I believe in God, the Father almighty," is much more akin to taking wedding vows, of promising "to love and to cherish, for richer, for poorer, in sickness and in health, and forsaking all others." This is what it means to say, "I believe in God, the Father almighty."

Belief, in the matter in which I speak here, is about love. Rather than the assent of my mind to a set of principles to be taken as "fact," belief is about the giving of one's heart to another understood as loving and trustworthy beyond question. But if that is so, how can we reconcile God as one to whom we give our hearts with the creed's identification of God as both "Father" and "almighty"? The two can seem incompatible to the contemporary mind.

I have had the pain and pleasure of being a human father for more than thirty years. My own Dad has carried that privilege and burden for far longer! What I can tell you is that neither one of us knows anything about being almighty. My children have rebelled against my admonitions, directives, orders, advice, and counsel, rendering me frustrated and angry, sad, tearful, and helpless. Likewise, I know I have caused my Father grieving, sorrow, and disappointment by my willfulness, headstrong ignorance, and outright refusal to listen to anything he had to say. But had either he or I tried to act with an almighty tyrannical hand over our children in such times, dominating over them and intimidating them, it would have proven fruitless. To do so either destroys the child, or it destroys the relationship and thus annihilates fatherhood.

Human fathers cannot reconcile in their persons being father and being almighty, because as humans we are constitutionally unable to wield almighty power in love. That brings me to the second realization of how my fatherhood is not almighty. I have failed my children. I have not been attentive to them in times when they were most in need. I cannot be omnipresent, and I have chosen to be somewhere else at times when they needed me to be with them. I have failed them because I cannot fully know their needs; I can only approximately meet them. I have, at times, been physically present and emotionally unavailable. I can identify many ways in which I have failed my children as a father, and I can tell you about many times when my father has failed me.

We are able to reconcile the Creed's identification of God as "Father almighty," because we cannot speak of God as almighty apart from God's fatherhood. We only know God's almightiness as God is almighty in parental love.

In the school I attended as a fifth-grader, I was classmates with a boy whose father was arrested for burglary. I knew a little about the family, and even as a ten-year-old I knew they didn't have it easy. Whatever the cause for their circumstances, Charlie's father lost heart and decided that the way out of poverty for his family was to steal someone else's money. He was arrested within two days of the burglary. The news of his arrest quickly made the local paper. The shame and ridicule Charlie experienced at school from other children, as well as the absence of his father, left him in tears and alone on the playground at recess. Perhaps Charlie's dad hadn't been a good provider, but he never really failed his family until he lost heart and turned to stealing.

Unlike with human fatherhood, God's heart does not fail us. God is ever-present to us, knowing our needs better than we can know them ourselves. So it is that in the liturgy for Holy Communion, the celebrant declares, "When our love failed, [God's] love remained steadfast." In our finiteness and human frailty, we are inconstant. God's love does not waver. God is ever constant toward us.

Secondly, God's all-mightiness is never exercised over us as tyranny or intimidation. God does not crush us when we disregard God's guidance and counsel. God's love remains steadfast when we choose to rebel. God does not disown us, even though we might disown God. We can take our inheritance early, run off to a far country and squander it on dissolute living and frivolities. If we should come to our senses and want to return home, we will not be met with the family patriarch who repeats, "I told you so," who demands an apology, remorse, and repayment. We will be met by the Father who runs out to meet us, falls upon our neck in love, welcomes us back into the family and throws the biggest bash ever seen (cf. Luke 15:11-32).

Some today will say that the gender-specific language of calling God Father is patriarchal and sexist. Didn't Jesus have a good relationship with Mary, his mother? Couldn't we speak of God as a nurturing mother? After all, the gender-specific image we use for God is based upon the parent who often isn't so God-like. I encounter this in counseling very often. People are confused about God, because they believe God is like their own father: cold, distant, and harsh — or worse: abusive, cruel, and abandoning. They say if God is that kind of father, they don't want anything to do with that God.

I believe there are good mother-images for God. Jesus speaks in motherly images as he laments over Jerusalem in Matthew 23:37:

"Jerusalem, Jerusalem, the city that kills the prophets and stones those who are sent to it! How often I desired to gather your children together as a hen gathers her brood under her wings, and you were not willing!"(RSV)

Mother-images for God can be helpful and they certainly are not inappropriate. The truth is mothers, too, fail their children and leave wounds that take a lifetime to heal. Both father-imagery and mother-imagery for God can lead us toward a dysfunctional faith based upon a human parent who was dysfunctional in their love and care toward us. Both have limitations with which we must wrestle and cope.

Some say why not jettison gender-specific language about God altogether? They advocate talking about the Trinitarian God we know as Father, Son, and Holy Spirit with the words, "Creator, redeemer, and sustainer." While these words do offer functional descriptions for the persons by whom we know the presence of God, they fall short of speaking in terms of relationship. We lose something very important in our understanding of God when we identify God only in functional terms. In sacrificing a relational understanding of God, we sacrifice something of our knowledge about ourselves and interacting with one another. For some, to say that speaking of God as Father is problematic is more than an understatement. Thinking in other relational ways about God the Creator is necessary, but not without some struggle of its own.

At the end of the day, Christians can only say that we speak of and to God as our Father because of Jesus. He lived in a

I Believe In God, The Father Almighty

patriarchal culture in which one's relationship to a father was the most significant relationship one might talk about. He spoke of and to God as "Abba," the Aramaic word children spoke when they sat on their fathers' laps and looked up into their eyes. As a grown man, that's the kind of intimate, tender relationship Jesus knew with God. The disciples envied him this relationship, and they wanted it. They overheard him in conversation with his heavenly Father, and they demanded, "Lord, John taught his disciples to pray; you teach us to pray." And so "he said to them, 'when you pray, say: Abba..." Father.

For Further Reflection

1. What do you mean when you say, "I believe in God, the Father almighty?"

2. Does the relationship you have had, or perhaps not had, with your father influence your understanding of God? Do you see this as a positive or negative influence? Does it accurately inform or distort your image of God?

3. Do you find the use of gender-specific language a hindrance to your profession of belief in God? Do you prefer another way of referring to the first person of the Trinity?

4. Someone has said that either God is all-mighty or God is all-loving, but God can't be both. How does professing that "God is almighty in love" correct that notion?

5. Do you find that your prayer life with God is intimate, or more formal? Is it more informed by "God the Father," or "God... the almighty?" Would you like to change something anything in that way about your prayer life?

Scripture for Meditation and Study...

Isaiah 63:15-19; Psalm 89:19-29;
Luke 15:11-32; Romans 8:12-16

Two

Creator Of Heaven And Earth

The argument continues to rage between evolutionary science and theistic creationism about how the universe and our world were formed. On one side are renowned scientists such as Richard Dawkins and Steven Hawking. On the other are Christian apologists such as Lee Strobel and Timothy Keller. The other day I drove past a local Christian bookstore that featured a large poster in the front window, which read, "Creation or Evolution? Come and Find Out!" The argument isn't confined to academic or publishing circles. Nor are the sides well-defined with atheistic scientists only on one side, and only professed Christians on the other. The question is a matter of some division within the church. Some Christians maintain that Genesis 1 should be understood literally. They say if you hold that it's a poetic metaphor that does not speak scientifically, the veracity of the whole Bible is made suspect. Others maintain that the Bible and science supplement each other, and are not contradictory or mutually exclusive.

I have no desire here to enter the fray between creationism and evolution. Others can publish books and fill the air with words on that front as they feel led — and perhaps their ongoing disagreement and debate is not unimportant. But my focus here is different. My objective in talking about the second part of the first clause in the Apostles' Creed is to uncover the common ground of belief we share as Christians when we profess belief in God the Father almighty as "Creator of heaven and earth."

The creed offers Christians a broad place to stand in charitable fellowship with one another despite dis-agreeing on matters that do not strike at the root of the faith. Thankfully, and I believe providentially, the Apostles' Creed does not bog down in details about how, during what period of time, or even for what purpose the universe came into being. It boldly and simply states that those who profess faith through the words of the creed believe in God as Creator of heaven and earth. What may we, then, authentically deduce about our profession from this sparse statement?

The first is that *God created all things.* In the words of Exodus 20:11, "the Lord made heaven and earth, the sea, and all that is in them." We can state no more, nor no less, than that. We maintain that we owe our existence, and the existence of all things, to God. We do not hold as necessary for salvation or make a basis for orthodox Christian profession any statement concerning whatever intermediate processes there may have been in God's creative work.

We simply assert that ultimately all things come from God.

Secondly, we may state that all things exist *by the sovereign will and creative word of God.* We cannot from the Apostles' Creed, which has its basis in scripture and the ancient teaching of the church, make any other dogmatic statement about the mode or means employed by God in bringing things into existence. The book of Genesis over and over again states the refrain, "And God said…." "And God said, 'Let there be light'; and there was light…. And God said 'Let there be a dome in the midst of the waters, and let it separate the waters from the waters'…. And God said, 'Let the waters bring forth swarms of living creatures'" (Genesis 1:3, 6, 20). This creative word of God is an expression of God's will. Go to the other end of the Bible, and the book of Revelation will depict the heavenly beings worshiping God as worthy of glory and declaring that it is because, "you created all things, and by your will they existed and were created" (Revelation 4:11). Christians may continue to differ from one another about the place of evolution or the views of creationism in the genesis of our universe, but we can agree that all things came into being according to the will and word of God.

Thirdly, we can confidently say in agreement that God the Father almighty, Creator of heaven and earth *created all things good.* I believe this has real implications for the daily exercise of our faith in stewarding the earth and its resources. We don't need to make care of the earth a crusade. It is a matter of routine daily life. In whatever way we can tread more lightly and more respectfully upon the earth, honoring that God loves all that God has made as good, the more we live in accord with the creed's profession of belief in God as creator of heaven and earth.

Little things matter. Picking up that errant piece of litter and disposing of it is significant stewardship. Using less water when we might thoughtlessly use more makes a difference. Recycling whenever possible, and buying with recycled and recyclable packaging in mind, contributes to care of the earth.

Little things do matter. I was reminded of this just the other day. I stepped out on my patio and heard a sparrow chirping in distress. I looked to see that it had somehow caught its leg in the fence and could not fly off. I was able to gently fold the bird into my left hand and guide its leg out of its dilemma with the right. The little sparrow was tiny. In the grand scheme of things, its life might be seen as inconsequential. But I remembered Jesus teaching his disciples and saying "Are not five sparrows sold for two pennies? Yet not one of them is forgotten in God's sight" (Luke 12:6). I released the sparrow and it quickly flew high into the trees. I believe in God the Father almighty, Creator of heaven and earth.

Finally, I believe the Apostles' Creed teaches that we are not self-made. We are a part of the good creation of God. We may be the apex of an evolutionary process, but we are not an evolutionary accident. For the scriptures tell us that we are created in the image of God. We might ask how it is that we have been created in the image of the unseen God. Many answers to this question have been proposed through the centuries. It has been said that humans having a capacity for discernment and making moral choices is the manner in which we are created in God's image. Others have said it is because we are the only one of God's creatures gifted with reason and the powers of self-reflection. These are true. But I believe above all, we know we are created in the image of God because we have the capacity for spiritual experience.

I believe God created the land and the air and the sea and all that is in them for his delight and enjoyment. But only human beings did God make for the purposes of communion and relationship. This, I believe, was God's desire in creating above all other desires. God loves all God has made, but whereas other creatures are loved, we are beloved: made for relationship, made

Creator Of Heaven And Earth

in God's image.

You know, it's always risky to love. Will our love be returned? And at what personal cost do we love another? God laid everything on the line — for us. God crossed the boundary between divinity and humanity — for us. God experienced dying and death — for us. We know God the Father as almighty in terms of creative love.

For Further Reflection

1. Do you believe the biblical account of creation in Genesis 1 and 2 needs to be understood literally? Do you think believing in the scientific theories of creation negates the possibility in believing in God as Creator?

2. Have you ever questioned your own existence? Do you ever ask why you are here? What does it mean for you, personally, to accept that you are here by the creative will of God?

3. How do you understand the belief that we are all created in the image of God? What difference does that make for how we treat one another?

4. Do you think learning more about the universe and theories of its genesis squeeze God out of the creative picture? Might growing scientific knowledge point toward a loving God?

5. What things are you currently doing to honor God's love of creation, including humans, plants, animals, and their environment? What other things might you be able to do that you currently aren't doing?

Scripture for Meditation and Study...

Genesis 1:1-2:9; Psalm 19; John 1:1-18;
Colossians 1:15-20

Three

I Believe In Jesus Christ...

For many years, my in-laws' family physician was Dr. Dodd. Dr. Dodd was well known in our area. He was born the son of medical missionaries in China. His office was in a wing built on to the house he and his wife occupied not long after his graduation from medical school. He stitched cuts, treated fractures, and delivered babies.

When I first came to know Dr. Dodd he was a man of advanced years, but still practicing medicine. He was a fixture, an institution, and if you asked anyone his full name, they all answered the same way: Dr. Dodd. No one knew if he had a real first name or not. He was never called "Doc" for short. It would have been disrespectful. He was Dr. Dodd. His title had become a part of his name. It placed him in our community, and it gave us a sense of his relationship to the rest of us.

In that part of the world in which Christianity is the dominant religion, we say the name Jesus Christ without thought that Christ is not a surname, but a title. Even by those who are completely secular, the man from Nazareth confessed as Lord by Christians is called Jesus Christ. But Christ is not a surname; it is a title. It is a translation of the Hebrew word messiah, which means chosen or anointed one. The word conjured a particular image in the Jewish imagination. The messiah was one coming who would reestablish the Davidic monarchy, purge the land of Israel of its occupiers and oppressors, establish an everlasting kingdom of righteousness, judge the nations, and vindicate the Jewish people.

The name Jesus was a common given name in first century Judaism. In Hebrew it was Yeshua, or as we say, Joshua. It means savior, or "one who saves." In Matthew, we read that Joseph was commanded in a dream to take Mary as his wife and name the child she was carrying "Jesus," for, the angel of the Lord told

I Believe In Jesus Christ...

Joseph, "He will save his people from their sins" (Matthew 1:21). His name places him among us. It gives us a sense of his relationship to us, and us to him. He is Savior and Messiah.

We rather much have domesticated him by casually taking his name and title upon our lips. We allow ourselves to say "Jesus Christ" the way we might say "Bill Jones" or "Jack Smith." For the earliest Christians, professing belief in Jesus Christ was not a casual statement. It was a profession that was religiously shocking and heretical. It set Gentile Christians apart from their pagan neighbors, because it separated them from the polytheistic religion and nature spirituality that typified pagan belief. Yet it also separated Jewish Christians from their former co-religionists, because it made a claim for Jesus that other Jews were not willing to make. It labeled Jewish Christians as heretics and outcasts from their roots.

Jesus Christ: Savior and Messiah. To profess belief in him might be something that in our own religious history is just a nice thing to do in church, but when the Apostles' Creed came into being as a liturgical profession made when one was baptized it was a radical act. It made very particular claims about a very particular person, and to own his name and title with conviction was seen as something religiously adversarial. Moreover, to say he is God's only son put one out on a limb even further.

Traditionalist Jews could in no way countenance the religious concept of the divine residing in a particular human person. The conviction that God is indivisible and wholly other separated their religion from all others. Romans and Greeks, on the other hand, had no problem saying the divine could be manifest in human form, but to believe that the divine would reside in the life of a common peasant — particularly a Palestinian Jewish peasant — was scandalous. An emperor might be divine, but not a carpenter!

Professing Jesus Christ as God's only son remains the scandal of particularity in our own day. In an increasingly pluralistic religious culture, it once again has taken on the tone of being an adversarial religious act. It subjects contemporary Christians to accusations of insensitivity and intolerance. Our profession of Jesus Christ as God's only son is not meant to shut down inter-religious dialogue, or to deny that truth can be found in other faiths. The openness we witness in Jesus toward a Roman centurion (cf. Luke 7:1-10) and a Samaritan woman (cf. John 4) sets a pattern for Christian dialogue with, and mutual respect for, religious viewpoints outside a Christian profession. Religious particularity is not a matter of exclusivity regarding interfaith conversation, but a place of spiritual location upon which we stand and from which dialogue with other faiths, for the good of all humanity, may take place.

A profession of Jesus Christ as God's only son is not necessarily adversarial, but it is a position of religious distinctiveness. Furthermore, in the global interfaith discussion it can become a position of mediation between spiritualties that locate the divine in everything material and those who place the divine completely outside of the physical world. Our profession of Jesus Christ as God's only son agrees, to a point, with those who believe that the divine is present everywhere in the material world, but also has a point of agreement with those traditions that place God forever outside of the created order. To deny the divinity of Jesus Christ or conversely to soft-peddle his distinctiveness as divine, eliminates rather than enhances the Christian position in contemporary interfaith conversations.

If the profession of Jesus Christ as God's only son was a religiously radical statement by early Christians, the profession of Jesus Christ as Lord was a politically dangerous one. While modern culture views the profession of Jesus as Lord as obscurantist and even quaint, it was not so viewed in the first and second centuries. It was a statement in defiant opposition to the Roman demand that Caesar, and no other, was lord of all.

The early twentieth-century British Christian, Sir Arthur Lunn, satirized superficial understandings of the gospel and marginal Christianity by paraphrasing John 3:16 with the words, "God so loved the world that he inspired a certain Jew that there was a great deal to be said for loving your neighbor."[1] That's a long way from professing Jesus as Lord in opposition to the greatest political power of the time.

Many of today's political and economic entities, including America and its economic establishment, allow that professing Jesus Christ as Lord is perfectly acceptable — providing you

1 Quoted by E. Stanley Jones in *Abundant Living*, ed. Dean Merrill (Minneapolis: Summerside, 2010), 208.

I Believe In Jesus Christ...

don't mean anything substantive by it. But the profession of Jesus Christ as Lord is meant to be politically and culturally substantive. We do not place our ultimate trust and loyalty in any government or political party — liberal or conservative, democratic, monarchical, or martial. We are not sworn to uphold any economic system, whether capitalist, communist, socialist, or feudal. Our primary citizenship is in another realm.

We can, and do, participate in worldly systems of governance and economics. We buy and sell, vote, and speak out on issues of significance to us. But our profession that we believe in Jesus Christ, God's only son, our Lord, calls us to always do so from a Christian perspective of ultimate loyalty to the principles of the reign of God — the kingdom for which we pray to be made manifest on earth, as in heaven. Our buying and selling is sympathetic to fair pay and treatment of those whose labors provide our goods. It is in accord with a sense of the need of others and our privileged position as consumers. Our participation in the political process reflects our concerns for equality, peace with justice, and an understanding of all nations and races as God's children.

The Apostles' Creed, for all its familiarity and rote recitation, remains a radical statement of faith. It is challenging but respectful of other religious traditions. It remains sternly oppositional to all political and economic systems that would deny or blunt our loyalty to the reign of God. I believe in Jesus Christ, God's only son, our Lord.

For Further Reflection

1. Do you believe it is necessary to profess Jesus Christ as "God's only son" in order to be a Christian? Why, or why not?

2. How might you respond, personally, to a charge that your profession of Jesus as God's son is exclusionary to people of other faiths and no faith? Is it possible to maintain Jesus' particularity in conversation with people of other religions and no religion?

3. Does calling Jesus the Christ still convey any meaning to you about who Jesus really is? Is the title Messiah more helpful? What appellation helps you most to relate to Jesus? Do you relate more to Jesus as Savior? Lord? Rabbi?

4. Do you find professing Jesus as Lord a radical commitment? Does it in any way force you to rethink other loyalties and commitments? Should it?

5. If you take professing Jesus as Lord more seriously, what routine things, like what you buy and who you buy it from, might you need to reconsider?

Scripture for Meditation and Study...

Micah 5:2-5a; Psalm 110; Mark 8:27-30; Acts 2:22-36

Four

Conceived By The Holy Spirit...

I have found it odd that hardly anyone, anywhere I have served as pastor has asked me about my theology. I had an ordination exam where I had to respond both in writing and verbally to questions about what I believe, but I don't ever recall being directly asked by a parishioner about my personal beliefs — except on one particular doctrine.

I have been asked on more than one occasion if I believe in the virgin birth of Jesus. On occasions when I have been confronted by this question, it was posed in a confrontational way, as a litmus test. And it has been posed to me as a litmus test by both conservative believers, who had decided not to accept me as their pastor if I did not confess a literal belief in the virgin birth, and by liberal believers, who had decided that if I did confess a literal belief in the virgin birth, they would right me off as an intellectual bumpkin.

My answer to the question has always proven somewhat unsatisfactory to everyone who has asked. I answer that I can recite the Apostles' Creed without qualms, but that I do not believe the creed is concerned with gynecology, but theology. I am usually then accused of being evasive. I don't mean to be. I think the creed is adequate as a theological statement. I also believe it is a statement of faith that sets Christianity apart from other faiths and no faith, but it was never intended to be an instrument of division within Christianity.

The creed does identify the mother of Jesus as "the virgin Mary," but I believe we might be putting "the em-*phá*-sis on the wrong syl-*lá*-ble," as my tenth grade grammar teacher used to tell us. In saying the Apostles' Creed, we profess that Jesus "was conceived by the Holy Spirit and born of the Virgin Mary." We twenty-first-century Christians have gotten all focused on the second part of that statement, when the evidence from the New Testament and church history seems to indicate that Mary the mother of Jesus and the story of the virgin birth was not a primary concern.

First off, the gospels mention Mary only in passing. In two of the four gospels there is no birth narrative at all. In Mark's gospel, we see Jesus repudiate his mother and brothers when they come out to take charge of him (Mark 3:31-35). Mary is absent from Jesus' passion and crucifixion in Matthew, Mark, and Luke; only the gospel of John has the mother of Jesus present at Golgotha.

Secondly, the nativity stories in Matthew and Luke are not really centered on Mary. Matthew gives Joseph a more focused role in the birth of Jesus than he gives to Mary. Matthew is concerned to proclaim Jesus as God's Messiah *from birth*. Jewish Christians understood the title "Messiah," and relied on Matthew's testimony that Jesus' birth fulfilled the words of the prophets. Gentile Christians, on the other hand, better understood the title "Son of God." Their faith in Jesus was vindicated by the story of Jesus' conception by the Holy Spirit, as Luke told it. But both Matthew and Luke are concerned with theology, not biology. They are focused on Jesus' spiritual origin in God, not in obstetrics.

Let me tell a story that I think speaks to where I am focusing.

My father was an automobile mechanic by trade. When I was a young, he taught me three primary things about automobiles. The first was that I should not consider auto mechanics as a trade unless I wanted to starve to death! With that out of the way, he went on to say that the internal combustion engine really isn't all that complicated. It only has two primary systems: fuel and electric.

Dad practiced the trade when fuel in a gasoline engine was delivered via a carburetion system, which was perhaps more complicated, if less efficient, than today's fuel injected cars. Dad taught me that 90% of minor engine malfunctions were electrical in nature. However, he said most novices and even a few professional mechanics always want to focus on the fuel system and tinker with the carburetor. He used to get frustrated when someone would bring him a car that wasn't running right and ask him to fix it. The problem would be spark plugs, wires, or some other component of the electrical system. He would correct the problem in the electrical system, only to discover the car still wouldn't run right because the owner admittedly had tried to adjust the carburetor first.

I asked him why people looked at the wrong thing first. He shrugged and said he thought it was because most folks could see gasoline and therefore were comfortable fooling with the fuel system. They really couldn't see electricity. They were frightened of power they could feel, but that was invisible to the eye.

The Apostles' Creed declares belief in Jesus, who was "conceived by the Holy Spirit, born of the Virgin Mary." Only two parts, but we get focused on the wrong thing. The theological point made is that Jesus "is the messianic Son of God and the Lord of the messianic kingdom not only since his resurrection from the dead, and not merely since his baptism by John the Baptist in the Jordan, but by his heavenly origin and from his earthly beginnings. It was not only Jesus' ministry which was *in* the power of the Holy Spirit. He springs from the very beginning *from* the power of the most high, the Holy Spirit."[2]

We tend to get obsessed with the game of "Virgin Birth: Fact or Fallacy." That's because we moderns imbibe of the seventeenth-century enlightenment bias toward reason and the scientific method. We are far more comfortable speaking in literal ways and in terms of biology than we are comfortable with poetry and symbolism — the primary language of early Christian theology. This is true of both liberal and conservative believers. We both want to talk in terms of the literal and physical. We just do it from opposite ends of the Enlightenment thought continuum, which is a straight line between yes and no without depth or any variation of shade in meaning. The Apostles' Creed speaks in an ancient way that is not one-dimensional, but rich, layered, and poetic. Its language will not submit to our literalism and either/or thinking.

The physical we can touch, examine, make bold statements about in flat, factual ways, whether favoring the skeptical or the supernatural. So we stay on the physical side, talk gynecology, and ask, "Do you believe in the literal virgin birth?" But we are a lot less comfortable using poetic imagery to talk theologically, to consider the otherwise unseen power of God walking among us, loving us, sharing with us conversation, laughter, fellowship,

2 Jurgen Moltmann. *The Way of Jesus Christ* (London: SCM Press, 1989). p. 81.

death — and holiness of all things. That kind of stuff is just too scary to fool with!

So, do I believe in the virgin birth of Jesus? My answer is that I can recite the Apostles' Creed without any qualms, but I do not believe the creed is making a physiological statement about Mary; it is making a theological statement about Jesus. And I think that is a better answer than the question typically deserves.

For Further Reflection

1. Have you ever been "quizzed" concerning your beliefs about Jesus' conception? Have you ever "quizzed" someone else about this in order to draw a conclusion about what kind of Christian the person is?

2. Do you think literal belief in the virgin birth as a biological fact is essential to be a Christian? Why, or why not?

3. Why do you think the gospels of Mark and John do not include a birth narrative about Jesus' origins? What makes the nativity narratives important for the theology (belief about Jesus) of Matthew and Luke?

4. What is important to believe about Mary regarding the person of Jesus? Do you believe she was sinless, or perhaps morally purer than other women? Does she need to be either of those to become the mother of the Messiah? Why, or why not?
5. Do you think it would be possible for Jesus to be "Son of the most high God" without being conceived miraculously?

Scripture for Meditation and Study...

Isaiah 7:10-17; Psalm 2; Matthew 1:18-25; Galatians 4:1-7

Five

Suffered...Crucified...Buried

As a high school student I was involved in an interdenominational youth group called Campus Life. Campus Life is a high school version of the evangelical college campus ministry called Campus Crusade for Christ. Now, you may be unfamiliar with these independent ministries, whose mission is to share the gospel with students. I can't say that I agree with everything Campus Life and Campus Crusade for Christ promote. However, I can say the Campus Life ministry I participated in was a major influence in my spiritual journey.

As a high school senior, I was very active in Campus Life. The leaders, or campus missionaries, were recent graduates of a local Christian college, and they were keenly interested in getting me to make a public profession of Jesus as my Savior. I was, frankly, a little flummoxed by this since I had grown up in the church and knew Jesus. I will admit that I was spiritually seeking, but the Campus Life leaders had diagnosed this as a need for an evangelical conversion. No one twisted my arm, or dragged me to a revival service with a mourner's bench, but these two evangelical student missionaries did remain engaged with me.

I remember well the climax of this spiritual drama. One day at a Campus Life outing, some questions I raised about Jesus' death on the cross led to a one-on-one with one of the Campus Life missionaries. I remember how he diagrammed things for me. He drew a picture of two cliffs with a wide chasm between. On the precipice of one cliff he drew a stick-figure representing me. On the other cliff he simply wrote the word, "God." After talking about how our sin alienates us from God, how the chasm in his picture represented that state of alienation, and how we can do nothing to bridge that chasm on our own, he drew the cross as spanning the chasm and on the cross he wrote the name, "Jesus."

I guess that was supposed to answer my questions about Jesus' death on the cross and what it means and what it accomplishes, because after the missionary finished with the lesson he asked me if I understood. I nodded that I understood what he had done, which didn't necessarily mean he had answered my questions. At any rate, as soon as I said I understood he asked me if I wanted to pray the salvation prayer. He was rather flummoxed when I told him no. I understood what he was telling me, but my questions still weren't answered.

Thankfully, with some time I came to know that I don't have to have all my questions answered about the cross in order to accept it as the sign of God's most profound gift of steadfast love. In fact, my questions still aren't all answered and perhaps never will be. Nonetheless, something reverberates deep in my soul when I say those words we find in the Apostles' Creed: "suffered under Pontius Pilate, was crucified, died and was buried; he descended to the dead." The once Archbishop of Canterbury, William Temple, wrote, "if any man says that he understands the relation of deity to humanity in Christ, he only makes it clear that he does not understand at all what is meant by an Incarnation."[3] I might echo that sentiment concerning the atonement of Christ by saying that anyone who says he understands everything accomplished in the cross makes it clear that he does not understand at all what is meant by atonement.

If you look up atonement in a theological dictionary, you might see the word broken down into its syllables as "at-one-ment." It generally means the "the restoration of the broken relationship between God and humanity accomplished in the life and death of Jesus Christ."[4] Looking back, I guess the Campus Life leader's diagram of the cross and the chasm wasn't a bad representation after all. However, I had questions about exactly how this happens in the cross. When we start asking questions about how our atonement is accomplished in the cross, we encounter three historical theories that have come to divide Christians from one another according to which theory is accepted.

One of these theories, and perhaps the most widely accepted

---

[3] William Temple. *Christus Veritas*, (New York: Macmillan, 1926). 139.
[4] Van A. Harvey. *A Handbook of Theological Terms*, (New York: Simon & Schuster, 1964). 33.

among evangelical believers in the western world, has been summarily titled the substitutionary theory. It basically states that you and I deserve the wrath of a righteous God poured out upon us for offending the divine majesty through our sinful disobedience and rebellion. However, the divine love of God sends the son, Jesus Christ, who takes our place. Jesus receives the full wrath of God in his own person, so that we might be forgiven and reconciled to God. Jesus acts as our substitute. This theory takes a strongly objective view of atonement as God's work on our behalf. It has its roots in the practice of scapegoating on the Day of Atonement, which we read about in the sixteenth chapter of the Old Testament book of Leviticus.

The second major theory has been termed the moral exemplar theory. The liberal Christianity of the nineteenth and early twentieth centuries favored this theory, and it continues as the favored theory within most of Eastern Orthodox Christianity. It has roots in early Christian reflection on the meaning of the cross. The basis of the moral exemplar theory is that God desires the transformation of our inner being, so that we repent of sin and turn to acceptance of God's love for us. The moral exemplar theory contains a more subjective element, focusing on a moral change necessary within us to make the act of atonement effective. God becomes incarnate in the person of Jesus, and as we are influenced by his teaching, sacrificial self-offering, and resurrection as an example of perfect love, our hearts are changed. From this conversion, we grow more and more into the image of Christ.

A third theory of the atonement is called the ransom theory. It views the meaning of the crucifixion as the means by which the powers of evil were defeated and the dominion of evil over human life broken. It, too, has its roots in ancient Christian reflection on the meaning of the cross, and probably draws some of its thinking from the culture of Western Europe after the fall of the Roman Empire. Basically, it sees the self-offering of Jesus as the means by which our lives are ransomed from the powers of sin, evil and death that hold us in bondage. His resurrection after surrendering to these powers demonstrates their ultimate weakness and moral bankruptcy, thus defeating them. After 1,000 years as perhaps the most widely accepted theory of atonement, the ransom theory fell out of favor with the development of the first theory I mentioned. However, this theory has gained ground in recent decades, especially within what has come to be known as the liberation theology movement, which is strong in many third-world countries and among the oppressed.

Which theory of the atonement makes sense to you? I think it really depends upon your personal history and human experience. I believe each theory contains something of the truth about the meaning of the cross. However, as I mentioned, my questions about the cross still aren't answered after all these many years of following Jesus. I don't think they will ever be answered, because I don't believe any theory of what Jesus accomplished for us on the cross can exhaust the meaning of that most profound and stunning event in history.

Should we make the acceptance of a particular theological theory the basis of what defines a Christian, what decides if we will be in fellowship with another believer? I know that I favor the meaning offered by the ransom theory of atonement, but I was educated in a seminary that promoted the study of liberation theology. I came of age in an era when third-world nations won their independence from colonial powers, and when the iron curtain fell and the former soviet republics became democracies. However, I do not hold those who favor other theories as believing wrongly because I confess that my understanding of the meaning of the cross remains partial. At its core, it remains a divine mystery. What I do know is, that in my core I experience cleansing, freedom, and transformation in professing simply with the Apostles' Creed that Jesus "suffered under Pontius Pilate, was crucified, died, and was buried."

For Further Reflection

1. Which theory of the atonement most resonates with you, personally? Why?

2. Do you find any of the most popular theories of the atonement off-putting? Why?

Suffered... Crucified... Buried...

3. Do you believe that "atonement" is even really necessary for us? Why, or why not?

4. Some Christians would say "Jesus saves!" is the primary message. Others might say it is "The Lord is risen," signifying Christ's victory over death. Does one of these resonate more with you than the other?

5. If you believe a person must adhere to one particular theory of atonement, which one is it? Why?

Scripture for Meditation and Study...

Isaiah 53:1-12; Psalm 22; Luke 23:26-56; Philippians 2:5-11

Six

The Third Day He Rose From The Dead

Ask a philosopher of history about the truth of the resurrection of Jesus, and you will probably be told that, philosophically, the resurrection is not historical. If you ask why the resurrection cannot be considered historical, you will be told that the resurrection cannot be comprehended according to the laws of historical inquiry.

On the other hand, if you ask a Christian theologian if the resurrection is a myth, you might not immediately get "no" for an answer. Instead, you might be asked what you mean by myth. If you mean a completely fallacious fabrication of a creative mind, then no — the resurrection, according to theology, is not a myth. But if you mean by myth that the resurrection is an inexplicable phenomenon of ultimate significance that defies historical and scientific explanation, the theologian might smile an affirmation back at you.

Former Secretary of Defense, Donald Rumsfeld, is quoted as saying: "There are known knowns. These are things we know that we know. There are known unknowns. That is to say, there are things that we know we don't know. But there are also unknown unknowns. There are things we don't know we don't know." It's too bad Mr. Rumsfeld was speaking at the time about the war in Iraq, rather than the gospel accounts of the resurrection of Jesus. A riddle seems a poor explanation for military strategy, but it might be a perfect explanation for why the gospels don't line up perfectly, keep the story straight, and present an airtight historical case for Jesus being raised from the dead. Instead, you have discrepancies about who got to the tomb first and did what. You have mystery.

No one saw Jesus being raised; the gospels tell of his disciples seeing him after he was raised. Where did Jesus first appear to

The Third Day He Rose From The Dead

his disciples after the empty tomb? Was it in the upper room, or in Galilee? It all depends on which gospel you reference. In one story, the resurrected Jesus warned Mary that he could not be touched. In another story, he invited his disciples to touch him, to feel his crucifixion wounds. In some accounts he was recognized immediately; in others, his true identity seems hidden at first. He ate a solid meal with his disciples, right after he entered the room without using the door. He appeared at table, and then vanished. So regarding a case for the historical fact of Jesus' resurrection, we don't have the kind of evidence or eyewitness testimony necessary.

So we might have to concede that according to the strict definition of history, the resurrection cannot be considered historical. But, we are not comfortable speaking of the resurrection of Jesus as a myth. We think of myths as stories we devise to explain events completely outside our knowledge of time and space. Such stories often include fictitious characters, places, and fantastical events. Many of us are comfortable talking about creation stories and heroic epics — even those included in the Bible — as mythical, outside of historical accounts, communicating human truths through fables and tales of legendary or even fictional characters — but the resurrection of Jesus? That's where we draw the line in the sand.

Many of us get a knot in our gut when we hear the resurrection of Jesus called, "the Christian myth." Yet, there are those church members who not only maintain that the resurrection can only be called a myth, but they will do so with the derogatory pronouncement that the resurrection is "just a myth." In other words, Jesus being raised from the dead is not only not historical to them, not only non-factual in the scientific sense, but it is fictional — an untruth.

I was the pastor of a congregation where one of my ministerial predecessors denied the resurrection of Jesus. It was a sardonic joke by some who remembered him that he could preach two Easter Sunday sermons and never once mention Jesus being raised from the dead. And this man left his mark on the church a generation later in the members who were influenced by his teaching and preaching, and had come to align their personal beliefs with his own.

I don't want to condemn those congregation members who

had struggled with the spiritual anxiety of trying to reconcile the resurrection and their formal education in the disciplines of empirical science and secular history. While I do not personally come out in my theologizing where they have come out, I still can appreciate the integrity of their struggle. And while they disclaim any belief in the resurrection of Jesus, many remain within the church and try to live out their discipleship according to their best understanding. Their problem, I think, is that they can't see an alternative between believing in the resurrection as historical event and regarding it as a complete and utter untruth. It is an "either-or" proposition for them, and their immersion in our secular scientific culture presents them with only one choice.

I can appreciate the integrity of their struggle, but I cannot concur with their conclusion. However, I have more empathy for those who have honestly rejected the claim of the Apostles' Creed, than for those who try to wash out the contradiction between history and myth by claiming the resurrection is a metaphor. In this regard, I have more respect for the honest unbeliever than for the metaphoric believer. I think Frederick Buechner beautifully captures my sentiments when he wrote:

> "We may try to say that the story of the resurrection means the teachings of Jesus are immortal like the plays of Shakespeare or the music of Beethoven. Or we can say that the resurrection means the spirit of Jesus is undying, that he lives the way Socrates does in the good he left behind.... We try to reduce it to the coming of spring, or the rebirth of hope in the despairing soul.... If I believed this was all the resurrection meant, then I would turn in my certificate of ordination and take up some other profession."[5]

We may accept the reality of the resurrection or we may deny its truth, but we are not given license to render it a vacuous metaphor for psychological improvement or human identification with the cycles of nature. There is a ground of belief between the resurrection as historical fact and the resurrection as Christian

---

5 Frederick Buechner, *The Magnificent Defeat* (San Francisco: Harper & Row, 1966), p. 77.

The Third Day He Rose From The Dead

myth, but that ground is not found in calling it a metaphor. We can call it a mystery, but not a metaphor.

How does one affirm that "on the third day he rose from the dead," and accept that such a claim is not historical? And how can we accept that the resurrection is not historical and yet deny that it neatly fits the category of myth? How do we spiritually stand in this gap?

For me, the answer can only be called the paradox of faith. I am trained as a pastoral theologian. I am also a student of history. The two are not antithetical, but each has something to contribute to Christian faith. Between historical fact and religious myth is the paradox of faith. Living with the paradox of faith requires us to accept that some elements of the resurrection story do not fit the definition of historical account.

The gospels do not agree in all of their details. They do not record eye witness accounts of the actual event of Jesus being raised from the dead. Yet, the gospels do not fabricate the characters who testify to experiencing the presence of Jesus after his crucifixion. The gospels do not spin fantastic yarns about the resurrected Jesus performing ghostly feats of superhuman prowess. There were, in fact, such stories written as gospels. But the early church rejected these stories as contrary to the truth. The canonical gospels record encounters of real people with the risen Lord in places you can find on a map.

The gospels avoid the fantastical, but they do not shy from the paradoxical. They speak of Jesus as bodily present, but whose body is different. He does very physical, material things such as sharing in food, only also to act in ways that are completely ethereal and metaphysical, such as appearing behind closed doors and disappearing from view after blessing and breaking bread. The early church did not try to smooth over the differences in the stories of the encounters with the risen Christ, or resolve the paradoxical nature of his appearances. It left the contradictions to stand, because it is within the contradictions — within the paradox — that faith lives.

Maybe you find the idea of paradox rather disconcerting. How can we be drawn to such utter contradiction? How can we believe in what cannot be proven? How can we live by what can only be described as mystery? Perhaps it seems absurd, but paradox is not illogical, because we know ourselves to be paradoxical in the very core of our being. We are rational beings, and we are emotional beings. We are historical beings who can never describe our lives in a purely historical way, because we can only relate our history by telling a story. Any time we tell a story, we tell it with mythical elements because we include our own perspectives and insights and interpretations, which are not historical. We each have a factual, personal history. We each have a personal myth. Together, they make us what we are: real, living beings.

So, if you ask me if the resurrection really happened, if you ask me if the resurrection is history or if the resurrection is a myth. My answer all the way around is a yes. It is the paradox whose truth we know by faith. I believe that "on the third day he rose again."

For Further Reflection

1. One Christian theologian wrote that if someone with a camera had been outside the tomb on Easter morning when Jesus rose from the dead, he would have captured the greatest photograph ever. Another wrote that the resurrection could never be photographed because it was not an event at all. What do you believe about these two statements? How can they be so disparate, while both theologians identified themselves as Christians?

2. Would you say that the resurrection of Jesus is a historical event? If so, how might you defend your belief to a secular historian?

3. What do you believe is signified by the word "myth?" Has the discussion above changed your mind at all about its meaning? If so, in what way?

4. Have you ever considered the differences in the accounts of the resurrection offered by the four gospels? What do you think accounts for these differences? Does the reality of differing accounts have an impact on your belief about the resurrection?

The Third Day He Rose From The Dead

5. Do you believe both myth and history are at work in the Christian profession of Jesus being raised from the dead?

Scripture for Meditation and Study...

1 Samuel 2:5-8; Psalm 18:4-19; Luke 24:13-35; Romans 4:16-25

Seven

He Ascended Into Heaven...

I had set aside some time to read books of Christian writers from the early twentieth century. As a historian and pastor, I have spent time reading patristic theologians and the works of the sixteenth century Protestant reformers. But, until rather recently, I had not considered the works of preachers and theologians of the twentieth century "historical." They didn't seem to have written that long ago. So, I read (or reread), people like Paul Tillich, Donald Baillie, Harry Emerson Fosdick, Leslie Weatherhead, Morton Kelsey, and E. Stanley Jones. You may be familiar with some of these men, and maybe not so much with others. Everything I read from them was written a few years before I was born. That's not a very long time ago, at least not in my thinking! Yet I find these authors use language differently than we use it today.

Authors writing in the first half of the twentieth century do not use gender inclusive language. They are much more sensitive than we are today to splitting infinitives, dangling participles, and ending sentences with a preposition. Their sentence structure is often quite different from what we are used to seeing from more contemporary writers. I also find that sometimes these earlier Christian writers will write about an event of their time with which I'm not familiar, or will use cultural idioms that are no longer current. Their worldview is different from my own, even though our lives may be separated by less than a century of time.

If I want to really understand what a writer was talking about, I sometimes have to stop and do some research. I have to find out about the event they wrote on, or look up the use of a now-defunct saying. But I take time to do that, because it's not really the author's words I'm after — although some of them use words in prose in a very poetic and flowing away. It's the author's mind

He Ascended Into Heaven...

that I want to know. I want to get in touch with his thinking, his religious insight, and his spiritual experience. That's really what I'm after when I read.

When I profess belief that Jesus "ascended into heaven" and "is seated at the right hand of the Father," I am fully aware that I am using language that was familiar and accurate to the worldview of people in the earlier years of the Christian era. They saw the universe in simple terms. At the center of it all was the earth: a flat, pancake-like abode for creatures, with the sky inverted over it like a huge bowl. On the surface of that bowl traveled the sun, the moon, and the stars and above it was heaven, where God was and to which the soul departed after death. So when the presence of the risen Christ departed from the disciples in a numinous spiritual experience, what categories and language could they use to describe that event other than "he ascended into heaven"?

What we read in the gospels does not provide a uniform account of the apostles' experience of the risen Jesus after the resurrection. Matthew's gospel ends with the great commission. John's gospel ends with the story of Peter's lakeside rehabilitation. The longer ending of Mark's gospel agrees with what Luke wrote about Jesus being taken up into heaven. Like with the resurrection accounts, there are discrepancies.

Undoubtedly Jesus' risen presence after death, his departure from his disciples, and his return to them in the form of the Holy Spirit are closely related experiences. For some, meeting the risen Jesus was an affirmation of his victory over death and evil. For others, there was a quality of finality and farewell to the experience. For some, it was a meeting that brought new spiritual energy and vitality. Perhaps for some all of this was one overwhelming experience, while for others it came as separate experiences. The church, in its worship and its creedal affirmations, has followed the separation of these three experiences as we find them in Luke's gospel and the Acts of the apostles.

When we say the Apostles' Creed today, we use language and concepts current at the time of its formation to affirm the spiritual reality of the experiences of the earliest followers of Jesus. We affirm that after a time of experiencing Jesus as alive and personally present after his crucifixion, he departed from the apostles and returned to God. And this all begs the question: so what? What bearing does this have on our Christian faith today?

First of all, it affirms for us the cosmic and permanent aspect of Jesus' incarnation. He did not assume human nature for a brief time — perhaps thirty or so years — and then shuck his humanity like a worn out suit. He returned to the spiritual realm of God bearing our humanity and uniting it forever with divinity. This is the final act in the drama of the atonement. There is no real "at-one-ment" without the divinization of our humanity through Jesus' return to God. When we say "he ascended into heaven, is seated at the right hand of the Father," we employ ancient and honored language and concepts to affirm that we have been reconciled to God.

We might stop right here overwhelmed by the sense of grace affirmed in this statement. Through this phrase in the Apostles' Creed, we resonate with that sense of awe expressed by Paul in Romans where he wrote that Jesus "was handed over to death for our trespasses and was raised for our justification," and "who is at the right hand of God, who indeed intercedes for us" (Romans 4:25; 8:34). Yet, I believe there is more to be inferred from this part of our statement of faith. There is another faith to be cherished, and a response to be made to it.

The risen Jesus bids his followers farewell, and leaves them with a notion of the reign of God to further define, to live out, to demonstrate, and to invite others to join and become subjects of. He bequeaths to us his mission and departs. He is no "micromanager"! He puts the church in charge of what he started. It is a radical act of faith on the part of Jesus, on the part of God. It is an act of faith in us, in you and me, in the church of all ages and places that we will continue in the way, that we will continue to do what Jesus did. Whenever we profess that we believe "he ascended into heaven, is seated at the right hand of the Father," we profess we believe God believes in us. We profess faith in God's faith in us.

Our response to such faith is an awesome responsibility. We are called not only to live in the light of Jesus' love, but also to reflect that love to others. We are called to follow Jesus in imitation of him; in obediently living out his commandments. "Thus you will know them by their fruits. Not everyone who says to me,

He Ascended Into Heaven...

'Lord, Lord,' will enter the kingdom of heaven, but only the one who does the will of my Father in heaven" (Matthew 7:20-21). "In everything, do to others as you would have them do to you, for this is the law and the prophets" (Matthew 7:12). "If you love me, you will keep my commandments" (John 14:15). These but outline the beginning of our response in believing in Jesus' belief in us.

Yes, our response to Jesus' belief in us is an awesome responsibility. It is, in fact, an impossible task if we think we can take it up all on our own. It is a futile thought without the knowledge that we are, in Jesus, united to God and the divine power of God forever. Furthermore, we are not only representatively taken into God's presence. Jesus' return to God signals the reciprocal action of God's continuing presence with us in the gift of the Holy Spirit. The incarnation continues on earth, even as it is in heaven.

The Apostles' Creed is a timeless affirmation wrapped up in archaic language. It reverences an experience of the apostles through ancient concepts. But we are not bound to the language or the concepts. It is not the words we want to get in touch with, but the spiritual experience. For the experience is continuingly relevant for living out the faith in our place and time.

For Further Reflection

1. What do you mean when you say that Jesus "ascended into heaven?" What image comes into your mind as you say these words?

2. What other ways might we talk about the risen Christ departing this plane of existent to enter into the fully spiritual realm of heaven? Translate? Migrate? Are any of these more helpful than "ascend?"

3. What difference does it make to you to believe that Jesus is just as human now, in the fully spiritual realm of heaven, as he was here on earth in a physical body?

4. How does it make you feel when someone says they have faith in you to accomplish something? How does it feel to believe that God has faith in you?

5. What do you need to do to be responsible today to God's faith in you?

Scripture for Meditation and Study...

Daniel 7:9-14; Psalm 47; John 20:11-18; Acts 1:6-11

Eight

He Will Come Again To Judge...

Our son, Andrew, has always been the most athletic of our three children. He played three sports in high school, continued to play baseball in college, and today is an avid golfer. I have been golfing with him when he has hit a hole-in-one. When his older brother and I golf with him, he consistently bests our scores by a number of strokes. Perhaps he is good at sports because he started young.

When Andrew was eight years old, he wanted to play little league baseball. Eight-year-olds were placed on a tee-ball team, where the ball is not pitched but hit off of a tee. Players learn to field, throw, and run the bases. In tee-ball games, no one keeps score. The idea is that young players simply play for the fun of being on the field.

"I do not want to play tee-ball," Andrew told the person registering players for little league. "I pitch and play shortstop. I want to play baseball." Andrew remained adamant about not registering for tee-ball. The league coaches agreed to let him try out for the minor league draft. If he proved he could compete with nine-and ten-year-olds, he could play at that level. Andrew showed that he could play at a level above his age, and was allowed to become a member of a minor league team, where they played by regular baseball rules.

I remember asking Andrew why he wouldn't play tee-ball. I thought it might be because he wouldn't get a chance to pitch — an element of the game his older brother and I had taught him in the backyard. But it wasn't that he couldn't pitch in tee-ball that was the problem.

"They don't keep score," Andrew said. "What's the use in playing if they don't keep score? If you don't keep score, nobody wins."

Certainly the competitiveness of youth sports has gotten out of hand in many ways. I can appreciate the spirit of little league tee-ball, where players are taught to love the game simply for the thrill of playing. Yet, I understood Andrew's point. Unless someone is tallying the innings and keeping score, nobody wins. Maybe nobody loses — but nobody wins, either.

We say as part of the Apostles' Creed that Christ "will come again to judge the living and the dead." I have an agnostic friend who feels the notion of the coming again of Jesus Christ as judge is more than a little dubious. When I was a parish pastor, he sometimes would ask how many were in worship in our church on Sunday. I would play along, and tell him how many were at early service and how many were at late service.

"You keep pretty accurate counts, don't you?" he would ask.

"Try to," I told him.

He would say something in response like, "Well, I guess that's important. Any God who is going to open that big book someday and judge who has been bad and who has been good is probably a stickler about attendance."

I'm sure a lot of earnest Christians look at the return of Christ and the final judgment something like that. We'll all line up and have our record reviewed, both those still living and those long dead and resurrected for the occasion, and we'll hope we've been good enough to have our tickets punched for that glory-bound train sung about in the old spiritual. I know many Christians, however, who believe a literal return of Christ and a final judgment of that mode is theologically questionable. Many of this type of believer sees the final judgment as something we might — might, mind you — face individually at the time of personal death.

I say might face at the time of personal death because they have a different viewpoint about this clause in which we profess belief that he "will come again to judge the living and the dead." They maintain an understanding of the final judgment that is more cosmic than individual, more about restoration than evaluation.

It doesn't take omnipotence to know that our world is out of whack from what seems to have been intended. We look around at the beauty of creation, the glory of diversity in the natural world, the values of goodness, truth and beauty that all human groups seem able to appreciate. We can see the universal condemnation human beings have placed upon greed, cruelty, avarice, murder, infidelity and we see how much those vices have infiltrated life. No, it doesn't take omnipotence and some kind of detailed final accounting at the end of history to know that things need to be different. Evaluation seems unnecessary.

In fact, we might even say that any evaluation in the final judgment is redundant. When the Savior of the world died in self-sacrificing agony, he there and then judged all human sin and evil. He took it to the cross and exposed it for what it is. Evaluation seems redundant, indeed. What we wait for in the final judgment is not evaluation, but restoration.

Restoration is what the apostle Paul foresaw in Romans 8. He spoke of it as that hope for things, which we do not see, but for which we wait with patience. He wrote of it as the freeing of a created order currently subject to bondage and decaying — a freedom that will be shared by all created things and that has its basis in the glorification of the children of God. The sin-stained will be cleansed. That corrupted by evil will be purged and made pristine. God will have wholly back again that which is rightfully God's.

It is interesting to me that the creed never adds what some informal and unofficial latter-day statements of faith have included. There is no statement to the effect that the just will be raised to eternal life and the unjust resurrected to eternal damnation. It doesn't really give us a hint about the content of a final judgment before the resurrected Lord.

It is true that Jesus, in the gospels, spoke of separating the sheep from goats (Matthew 25:31-46), of bridesmaids who join the great wedding banquet and those who do not get to enter (Matthew 25:1-13), and of those cast into outer darkness where there is weeping and gnashing of teeth (Matthew 22:11-14). But in these parables, the judged are at times a collective and at other times may be understood as individuals. And there is no mention of a fiery hell, or if the punishment received by those who are not included among the just is in any way eternal. We can infer that's the way Jesus intended to communicate it, but there can be a significant case made for saying that the punishment Jesus spoke of is remedial and not final. Repentance may still be a live option at the judgment.

Personally, I'm something of what might be called a "hopeful universalist" with regard to any final judgment. I'm hoping it is about restoration--a restoration of all things to full communion and harmony with God, as I believe God intended things to be for all that God created.

First of all, if that is true, then it means that my tendency to judge others is completely out of place. My proclivity for assigning those with certain behaviors or certain faults to the resurrection of the damned in my own thinking isn't just inappropriate. If the final judgment is about restoration rather than evaluation, it's not even relevant.

Secondly, it means the Christian hope is greater than we might first imagine. It means there may be hope for Mother Teresa and Adolph Hitler, for Dorothy Day and for Ivan the Terrible, for Saint Peter — and, yes, even for Judas Iscariot. For some of these I have named it probably means an awful ordeal of change and transformation. It might mean a rather fiery purging of their earthly personalities and cleansing of their souls that will be painful beyond imagining. I admit that my "hopeful universalism" may be mistaken. I could be wrong. If I am, I will someday stand corrected. But I remain confident that a loving God would not condemn me for mistakenly hoping that a way may be found for the worst examples of humanity to be restored to God.

Some may blanch at my hope that all will be restored to communion with God; that all will, at the coming again of Christ in judgment, be saved. Some might say such belief is returning to a notion of no winners and no losers, that it makes all of this meaningless. If in the final tally the righteous are not rewarded and the unjust are not cut off from life, then what's the point?

I believe that saying there are no winners or losers if a final judgment is restorative rather than evaluative is incorrect. Thinking that Christ's return in judgment is about our being rewarded or punished is what, in fact, misses the point. Because the point is that it's not about us. It's about God. It's about the yearning of God after all that rightfully belongs to God finally being fulfilled. It is about God getting God's way. In the restoration of all things to God in the return of Christ and the final judgment there is, indeed a winner: God is the winner.

He Will Come Again To Judge...

That's our hope. I believe Jesus Christ will come again to judge the living and the dead.

For Further Reflection

1. Does your church subscribe to an official confession or statement of faith? What does it say about Jesus' return and a final judgment? Do you personally agree with it?

2. Do you believe the everlasting damnation of the wicked is necessary to vindicate the righteous? Is it necessary to Jesus' sacrificial life and death? Why, or why not?

3. How might a belief in the final judgment as restorative rather than punitive impact your thinking about the goals and work of the criminal justice system? Are these two related in any way?

4. How do you understand what Paul is saying about the end of all things as he writes about it in Romans 8?

5. Do you think a restoration of all things to communion with God at the end of history can be in accord with God's justice without the eternal damnation of some people? Why, or why not?

Scripture for Meditation and Study...

Isaiah 11:1-9; Psalm 72; Matthew 25:31-46;
Romans 8:18-30

Nine

I Believe In The Holy Spirit

"I believe in the Holy Spirit." Sometimes I hurry through that part of the creed, hopeful that I don't allow my mind to linger too long on what I just said or meant by saying it. I stand spiritually within the Methodist tradition. We might well be called the first Protestant charismatics. One of the most serious criticisms of the theology of John Wesley was his insistence on the ability of the individual believer to have a direct experience of the presence of God in one's life. This insistence on a personal experience of God through the ministry of the Holy Spirit got Wesley and the early Methodists the derogatory appellation of "religious enthusiasts." It wasn't a good thing to be labeled a religious enthusiast in eighteenth-century England.

One of Wesley's most important sermons was titled, "The Witness of the Spirit," based on Romans 8:16, which read, "It is that very Spirit bearing witness with our spirit that we are children of God." In fact, this understanding of the Holy Spirit's ministry with us was so important to John Wesley that there are two installments of the sermon, "The Witness of the Spirit." In both sermons, Wesley insisted that the Holy Spirit comes to a believer personally and gives an inward assurance of one's saving relationship with God through Christ. This was considered a dangerous idea, because a believer so convinced of having the indwelling of the Holy Spirit might take it upon themselves to start speaking on behalf of God without the approval of church authority. This might lead to all kinds of religious conflict, when some people believing that an emotional experience of God's indwelling gives them power and authority without a measure of objective accountability. England had just been through a century of religious warfare, and keeping religion sedate and inoffensive was a primary concern. Religious enthusiasts were a

I Believe In The Holy Spirit

danger to spiritual tranquility!

My daughter is Episcopalian, if not by actual church membership at least by spiritual temperament. She dates a fellow who is Pentecostal. They find it difficult to go to church together. He finds the liturgical tradition of the Episcopal Church a strange vehicle for the Holy Spirit. She's afraid to go to a Pentecostal service with him, fearing that someone next to her might get slain in the Spirit or start speaking in tongues. Their spiritual differences are why when I say, "I believe in the Holy Spirit," in reciting the creed that I get more than a little uneasy. Trying to place myself on some sort of spectrum of belief regarding the activity of the Holy Spirit is difficult for me. The Holy Spirit is a danger to my spiritual tranquility!

In churches that I have pastored, I have sometimes been asked if I thought speaking in tongues was a real gift of God or if people "just fake it." It's obvious by the nature of the question that some skepticism lies behind it. I've never had the experience of speaking in tongues. However, my very best friend growing up became a Pentecostal preacher later in life, and testifies to the power of the Holy Spirit in his life and to the reality of speaking in tongues as an authentic part of his religious experience. I know my friend to be genuine. I have to believe there is something to it, although I don't know about it personally. I also remember when my friend was a quiet claims adjustor in California, for whom church was a fond memory from his childhood. Then he encountered God in a very real way in his life. The Holy Spirit certainly proved to be a danger to his spiritual tranquility!

Perhaps the main thing we can believe and know about the Holy Spirit is just this: perhaps it is the Holy Spirit's chief goal and activity to go about disrupting our spiritual tranquility. The Holy Spirit might just be the person of the Trinity charged with shaking us up, of shaking us out of our state of spiritual sedation.

The Protestant reformers of the 16th century, being so focused on the Bible as the ultimate authority for the church (rather than the pope) and the ultimate source of guidance for the rank-and-file believer (rather than church tradition), tended to tie the ministry of the Holy Spirit rather tightly to scripture. If it wasn't the Spirit's only ministry, being the divine muse for the writers of the sacred texts certainly was the Spirit's primary work. Secondarily, the Holy Spirit was understood as the power of God available to individual believers to read, interpret, and understand what God was saying through the Scripture. This might sound like pretty mundane and sedate activity. However, the notion that individual believers could interpret the Bible for themselves without the mediation and expertise of the clergy was considered spiritually dangerous by Roman Catholic Church authorities. After all, who was to say when the Holy Spirit was speaking through Scripture and when the individual reader was really hearing some other spirit of dubious origin? The whole idea could easily upset Christendom's spiritual tranquility.

It seems, then, that the problem in professing belief in the Holy Spirit is that in doing so we profess a need to surrender our lust for spiritual tranquility. I remember David Lowes Watson telling seminarians in congregational ministry courses to beware of falling into the comfortable role of pastoral pharmacist, doling out "spiritual amphetamines" to anesthetize parishioners against the work of authentic discipleship. Authentic discipleship really can't happen — at least not over the long haul — without the empowering activity of the Holy Spirit. It turns out that there is a healthy degree of spiritual dis-ease with which Christians ought to be moderately afflicted.

The germ agent, if you will, of healthy spiritual dis-ease is non-other than the Holy Spirit — the one who hovered over the waters of creation, the divine entity in Jesus conception who came upon him as he rose up out of the waters of baptism, the one who brings forth something from nothing, who raises the dead to life. Spiritual tranquility is the quest of hobby-Christians: people who desire the form without the power and disruption of godliness. For those seeking to drink more deeply of God and praying to live as authentic disciples of Jesus, the desire is to be overwhelmed by Holy Spirit infection and to throw spiritual tranquility to the wind.

No doubt we sometimes experience the Spirit as a gentle breeze, a warming of the heart as John Wesley is said to have experienced at Aldersgate. No doubt we can experience God's indwelling as a comforting reassurance of our place in the family of God, that we are children of the Father. But feelings about the Spirit are always penultimate to the reality of the Spirit's work in

I Believe In The Holy Spirit

us and in our world. It was the Spirit who brooded over the face of the chaos and brought forth a universe from nothing. It is the gift of the Spirit in the breath of Jesus that grants the awesome gift and responsibility of forgiveness and reconciliation. It is the Spirit who empowered a group of dispirited disciples to become a church bearing the promise that not even the gates of hell could prevail against it.

To parody the words of a veiled threat, the Holy Spirit knows where you sleep. The Spirit's presence always promises to smash our religious lethargy and to disturb our spiritual tranquility.

For Further Reflection

1. Do you pray for the Holy Spirit's help and guidance in understanding the scriptures before Bible reading? Is this something you might make a spiritual practice?

2. Someone has said that the Holy Spirit just seems like "a vague blur." Is that a remark you can relate to in your own faith?

3. Has the Holy Spirit ever disrupted your spiritual tranquility? If so, how? In what way?

4. Is it necessary to test if the Holy Spirit is speaking to someone through the scriptures to make sure it is not the voice of another spirit — perhaps a malevolent one? If so, how should that testing happen?

5. What is the relationship of the Holy Spirit to the community called church? How does that relationship get lived out in your congregation?

Scripture for Meditation and Study...

Numbers 24:1-14; Psalm 104:24-34; John 20:19-23;
Acts 2:1-13

Ten

The Holy Catholic Church

In a little rural parish where I served as pastor, the folks didn't like saying the Apostles' Creed. They didn't have any problem professing that Jesus was "conceived by the Holy Spirit, born of the Virgin Mary." They actually loved saying the phrase, "on the third day he rose from the dead." But right after saying, "I believe in the Holy Spirit," a lump formed in the throats of many of the members.

"Pastor, can't we say 'holy Christian church' instead?" they would ask. I knew what the problem was, but always being a little ornery, I asked why they didn't want to say they believed in "the holy catholic church."

"Because we aren't Catholic!" they would blurt out. And, again, being a little ornery, I would answer, "Oh yes, you are catholic!"

It was a teaching moment. I eventually relented to using the word "universal" in saying the creed in that parish, but I explained that Christian was not a synonym for catholic. I shared that our use of the word "catholic" in saying The Apostles' Creed was different than saying "Roman Catholic." I've come to appreciate the thought of liturgical scholar Laurence Hull Stookey on this subject. In the prayer book, *This Day*, as part of a devotional cycle focused on the marks of the church, Stookey wrote, "'catholic,' far from meaning one particular branch of the church, means the entire tree of the church." Stookey continued, "The Roman Catholic Church is that part of the universal church headquartered in Rome. But Protestant bodies could well argue that they are 'Lutheran Catholics' or 'Presbyterian Catholics,' for example."[6]

I looked up 'catholic' in my Webster's Dictionary to see

---

6 Laurence Hull Stookey, *This Day, A Wesleyan Way of Prayer* (Nashville: Abingdon Press, 2004), 86.

The Holy Catholic Church

a definition of the word. The first three definitions offered for catholic are:

1. of general scope or value; all-inclusive; universal
2. broad in sympathies, tastes, or understanding; liberal
3. of the Christian church as a whole; specif., of the ancient, undivided Christian church.[7]

The first definition is very much in accord with our substitution of the word "universal" for "catholic" in saying the Apostles' Creed. We are professing faith in the body of Christ around the world in its myriad of manifestations and expressions. We are talking all-inclusively within the scope of the Creed's profession of belief. So we are never professing ultimate faith in any denominational expression of the church; we are professing faith in the church against which the gates of hell will not prevail, with all of its differing forms of worship, governance, theological emphases, and spiritual gifts.

This leads us to the second definition that Webster offers for catholic: "broad in sympathies, tastes, or understanding; liberal." We probably need to start at the end of that definition with the word "liberal." Liberal has become a pejorative word in many religious, as well as political, circles. I think we need to understand that the word liberal suffers the same problem as the word catholic. We need to look at a well-focused definition of the word in its formal use, rather than connote it with all the baggage that has gotten attached to its use.

Liberal originally meant those characteristics belonging to a free people. Through time it came also to mean giving freely and generously, of largess, and of being plentiful and abundant. Only later did it come to be used to express negatively excessive tolerance, whether in economics, politics, or religious belief.

The christianity of the Apostles' Creed is liberal in the best sense of the word. It is "broad in sympathies, tastes, or understanding." The orthodox belief professed by the Apostles' Creed makes "the holy catholic church" a big tent encompassing variations of faith and practice, while defining and defending a non-negotiable core

---

7 *Webster's New World Dictionary, Third College Edition* (New York: Simon & Schuster, 1988), 222.

of Christian belief. To profess belief in "the holy catholic church" necessarily means we reject excessively narrow definitions of Christianity that unnecessarily exclude vast groups of folks from the worldwide body of Christ. I think I love the Apostles' Creed so much because it is a statement of faith meant to include, not exclude. If you can say it with integrity, I accept you as a fellow member of the body of Christ. I place no other stumbling blocks on our fellowship.

What about that third definition from Webster's? How can we ever profess belief in "the holy catholic church" if it means "the Christian church as a whole; specifically, of the ancient, undivided Christian church." How can we imagine the church is holy and catholic when it has experienced so many unholy rancorous schisms, disunity, and even murderous infighting? If you believe I exaggerate, you've never been to one of your congregation's council, board, or vestry meetings — depending upon what tradition you are part of! I jest, of course, but only a little.

Some scholars and observers of the church through history have liked to talk about "the invisible church." They postulate that the visible, worldly, institutional forms of the church cannot be equated with the true church. They define the true church as believers, scattered throughout different countries and congregations, committed above all to Jesus Christ without any loyalty adhering to a particular group. They maintain this invisible, true church — completely pure and without blemish — is the holy church, the church that the New Testament identifies as the bride of Christ.

The problem with this idea of a holy church, or "the true church," is that it's hard to see how a church with this definition of holiness has anything to do with the redemption of the world for which Christ died. How is such an amorphous group of pure, unblemished disciples a part of God's mission to redeem the world? I refer us to something written by martyred Archbishop Oscar Romero:

> "This is the mission entrusted to the church, and it is a hard mission: to uproot sins from history, to uproot sins from the political order, to uproot sins from the economy,

to uproot wherever they are. What a hard task!"[8]

That task of which Romero speaks is a holy task, but how could it ever be engaged by an "invisible church?"

Perhaps this all misses the point, because we are once again stumbling over the right definitions of words. When we profess belief in "the holy catholic church," we are not using the word holy in the sense of meaning exceptional goodness or purity. We can't speak of such holiness as existing within the created world as we currently have it. We can only speak of the holiness of God in such terms. When we speak of the church as holy, we are not making a claim about the purity or harmony of the church. We are speaking of holy as "being set apart." I'll give Webster's dictionary pride of place once again, which gives the first definition for the word holy as meaning, "dedicated to religious use; belonging to or coming from God; consecrated; sacred."[9] When we say the church is holy, we aren't talking anything about what the church does; we are talking about what God has done, is doing, and will do in and through the church.

I think Winchester Cathedral might be a good analogy for the holy catholic church. I'm thinking in particular of the Great West Window of that hallowed English edifice. The window is an immense work of stained glass, dominating the nave, and costing a small fortune when it was first built and installed in the early fifteenth century. Tremendously colorful, it included pictures of nobles, saints, and churchmen.

In 1642, the great window was destroyed in the English Civil War — ironically by the devout Puritan soldiers of Oliver Cromwell. Cromwell's troops, presumably offended by the show of worldly extravagance affected by the window, deliberately wrecked it by throwing at it whatever came to hand. But the glass fragments were painstakingly collected by the locals, and in 1660, when the monarchy was restored, they set to work putting the window back together. However, the difficulty of recreating the original design was just too great, and so the result is a rather haphazard reconstruction pre-figuring collage art by several

---

[8] Oscar Romero, *The Violence of Love*, trans. James R. Brockman (Farmington: Plough, 1998), pp. 29-30.
[9] *Webster's New World Dictionary, Third College Edition*, 644.

hundred years!

The great west window of Winchester Cathedral is today an abstract piecing together of broken glass. Saints' heads poke out here and there from among the collage of ruby, brilliant blue and gold glass fragments. And while it has little resemblance otherwise to what it was at its beginning, it still fills the nave with a diversity of beautiful color when the afternoon sun shines through it.

So it is with the church. It may be no coincidence that we call the church the body of Christ, and when we are offered the bread of Holy Communion it comes to us with the words, "the body of Christ, broken for you." The church is diverse but broken, pieced together but not unified, hardly identifiable with its original and yet made up from all that came before it. Despite its fragmentation, saints can still be spotted poking out here and there from its collage — and it still can bring color and life to the world whenever the light of the son shines through it. I believe in the holy catholic church.

For Further Reflection

1. Does your congregation use the Apostles' Creed regularly in worship? Do you say, "holy catholic church," or is there a word substitution made for "catholic?" How have you understood the word "catholic" in the past?

2. How do you feel about the above interpretation of the word "liberal" being related to the label "catholic" for the church?

3. Is an understanding of the term "catholic church" that includes many denominations and interpretations of faith too liberal? Why, or why not?

4. Do you believe the "holy catholic church" as you

The Holy Catholic Church

understand it today is not liberal enough? Who do you believe the church universal is unjustly excluding?

5. In what ways does cooperative ministry between denominations happen today that makes "the holy catholic church" a more visible reality? What more might be done in this effort?

Scripture for Meditation and Study...

Acts 2:37-47; Psalm 133; Matthew 28:16-20; Ephesians 4:1-16

Eleven

The Communion Of Saints

It's difficult for us in the comfortable setting of our churches with climate controlled sanctuaries and padded pews to remember that the first Christians worshiped in cemeteries. In pagan Rome, the church gathered in the catacombs — the burial chambers that lay beneath the city. We may think the primary reason was to hide from the prying eyes of authorities, but the truth is that Christians typically gathered in cemeteries for worship regardless of their address. It was a very real way of acknowledging belief in the communion of the saints and the ongoing fellowship of the living with the dead.

As with many practices of the early church, we later Christians have abbreviated the frequency of our formal observance of the communion of saints. In November, we observe All Saints' Day or All Saints' Sunday by reading the names of those from our community who have died during the previous year. Some congregations light a candle as each name is read; some ring a bell, and others simply allow the reading of the names to be enough. These are all good ways to symbolically observe our ongoing communion and fellowship with those who have died. However I believe current practice, which is little more than a tip of the hat to those who have recently passed through the veil of death, falls short of making real what the communion of saints is all about.

Professing belief in the communion of saints means we take seriously that our local-and-living community of faith is not the do-all and end-all of the church. We are claiming that the church is not defined or limited by space or time. In professing belief in the communion of saints we are committing to something far greater than ourselves. We are saying that, with regard to the church as the body of Christ, the whole is greater than the sum of

The Communion Of Saints

its parts. When we profess belief in the communion of saints, we are accepting a responsibility toward other Christians in other places — those who are dead, those who are living, and those who are yet to be.

The communion of saints is the spiritual connective tissue that links us in the body of Christ with Roman Catholics in South America, Anglicans in Nigeria, Orthodox Christians in Macedonia, and Presbyterians in Korea. We stand in solidarity with one another. We can have differing forms of governance. Some may look to leaders they call bishops, and pastors in a given denomination can agree to be directly accountable to one another. Some can hold a congregational polity, making the pastor accountable only to a council or board of the congregation. We can say church property is held in trust by the denomination, or owned by the individual congregation. What we can't do in any real way is declare that we are "independent" and still maintain that we are a part of the body of Christ. The church is always connected one congregation to another, one denomination to another, whether our idea of congregational government reflects that connectedness or not.

Nor is the church only the current living members of the body of Christ. When we observe All Saints' Sunday, we are not just honoring the past contributions of now-dead church members, or providing a communal mourning ritual for the living members of the church. We are saying that we believe those folks no longer seen are, in reality, still teaching us, still guiding us, and still an actual part of our fellowship. This is what the writer of the Hebrews wanted to communicate when he wrote about all the departed who had been martyrs and heroes of the faith, who now are a great cloud of witnesses cheering us on who are still alive and in the flesh (cf. Hebrews 11-12).

Sometimes just the word "saints" can get us a little confused. Some branches of the church hold up for veneration heroes of the faith, whose lives have been exemplary in living out the gospel in witness to Jesus Christ. Such folks are given the designation of saint. I think it's not a bad idea to honor with certain feast days and celebrations people like the great founder of Western monasticism, Benedict of Nursia, and Francis of Assisi who took to heart Jesus' command to sell all and give to the poor and come

Reconsidering the Apostle's Creed

follow him. In an age when the heroes of the culture are over-paid athletes, celebrities of questionable moral fiber, and entertainers whose greatest attribute is an ability to flaunt their wealth, the church could do a lot worse things than celebrate the heroes of the faith.

However, some of us do struggle with that title of "saint" for these heroes of the faith. It's confusing because it seems to set up a hierarchy of believers. Those of us whose traditions do not celebrate feast days for individual heroes of the faith have a different definition for the word saint. We are all saints, in that we hold that to be a saint is to be one called of God into the body of Christ. Holiness is a matter of God's claim upon us rather than our performance as a Christian. It's the same thought in which we considered the holy catholic church as being holy because of God's action in bringing the church into being instead of some kind of sanctity produced by the church's actions.

When we speak of the communion of saints, we talk about all of us including all who have gone before us in Christian faith and those who are still to be born into the faith. And as a body we are of sacred worth to God beyond the total of our individual sacredness to God as persons — even including those heroes of the faith that some branches of the church designate as "the saints." When we are baptized and taken into the body of Christ, we are given to something greater than ourselves. If the greatest commitment we have in life is simply to our self-preservation and self-aggrandizement, what an impoverished life that is! Thankfully, there is something within us that makes us yearn to be committed to something greater than our individual person. We want to be part of something grand. In my particular tradition, our baptismal liturgy once included the phrase, "The church is of God, and will be preserved to the end of time." What can be grander than the body of Christ?

A danger to an authentic profession of belief in the communion of saints is that we can allow it to devolve into a kind of sentimental attachment to the past. My home church was once named "Speddy Memorial Methodist Episcopal Church." Mr. Speddy was a leading citizen, the editor of the town's newspaper, a staunch Methodist, and a virulent prohibitionist. As much as Mr. Speddy was opposed to strong drink, he wasn't opposed to binge eating. A portrait of Mr. Speddy hangs in the main vestibule of the church, and it is obvious that he was a man of, shall we say, substantial girth. Local legend maintains that Mr. Speddy died at his editor's desk late one night after consuming a crock of chicken gizzards procured at a Methodist Church supper. The story holds that the empty crock was before him on the desk when his lifeless but well-fed body was discovered the next morning. Even given his unsavory demise, Mr. Speddy is venerated as a crusader against demon rum and a benefactor to the church, having given a great deal of money to construct the building that once bore his name "in memoriam."

That congregation's continuing communion with John Speddy is a sentimental one. It does nothing to empower its current faith and mission. Likewise, All Saints' Sunday observances may provide a positive time of remembrance. They may even help the community of the church process its grief over the loss of beloved members in a helpful way. However, such observances simply can be sentimentality that does not empower the ongoing discipleship of the body. It's important that our profession of belief in the communion of saints empower our faith now by helping us understand that we are responsible to one another, to those living Christians with us, to those who have gone before us, and those who are yet to be.

We have a responsibility to the saints we have loved but see no more, to actively live out the faith they have handed on to us. We are responsible for defining discipleship and faithfulness in our own time, just as they did in theirs. We have a responsibility to them to do what we can now and not simply recall their faithfulness with nostalgia for some golden age of the church, which, in fact, had its own problems, failures, and challenges. Crusading against alcohol abuse may have been the appropriate actions for John W. Speddy and his co-religionists. But in an era of rampant child sexual abuse, homelessness, and declining health care availability for many, our energies may be better spent in other calls to discipleship. That's what it means to believe in the communion of saints.

We have a responsibility to fellow Christians living now. We need to hold one another accountable in love, supporting each other in the journey of faith in whatever ways are appropriate.

Reconsidering the Apostle's Creed

We need to share our resources with Christians in need, whether they are halfway around the world, across town, or sitting at the other end of the pew. If Palestinian Christians are suffering because of the political turmoil in their land, we bear that wound. If African Christians are starving, we feel those pains of hunger. If an ethnic congregation has its church building burned as a hate crime, their tears are ours. If a family in our congregation is torn by domestic violence, we stand with the victims in the midst of their anguish. That's what it means to believe in the communion of saints.

We have a responsibility to Christians that are yet to come. Spiritual formation happens when we tell the stories of the faith in meaningful ways to a rising generation of Christians. I have been pondering what it would mean to simply turn children's Sunday school into story time. Instead of developing slick curricula for children with craft activities and hand puppets, what if we developed storytellers who could relate Bible stories with vividness and an energy that helped kids remember Moses at the burning bush and Joseph's many-colored coat? What if we could help adults tell the story of Samuel anointing David with wide eyes and a sense of suspense? What if we had storytellers who could make young people almost see the splendor of Gabriel before Mary at the annunciation? We have a responsibility to pass on to a rising generation the faith once delivered to the saints.

What if we mentored new Christians in discipleship? We could show them what it means to love one another as Christ loved us instead of just reading the passage out of the book. We can connect them with the blessing that is tithing one's living — not just money, as important as that is, but one's living. We could partner with them in volunteering at the food bank, or the literacy council, or the CROP Walk.

We can leave a legacy of nostalgia and sentimental observances, or we can leave of legacy of discipleship and handing on the faith. There are generations of Christians yet to come who need us to model and to pass on what it means to live into God's call to be a saint. I believe in the communion of saints.

The Communion Of Saints

For Further Reflection

1. Does your congregation observe All Saints' Day or Sunday? How? What positive benefit, personally and for your congregation as a whole, do you feel results from this observance?

2. Does Christian education in your church include teaching about past Christian "heroes of the faith," perhaps a denominational leader or founder, missionaries, or martyrs? What story do their stories tell?

3. What are some significant ways your congregation supports Christians in other parts of the world, particularly those who are in difficult circumstances? What further steps could be taken to acknowledge a connectedness between your congregation and other Christians?

4. Is there any fellowship or supportive connection between your congregation and other churches of various denominations in your town or city? In what ways is the communion of saints lived out through this group or organization?

5. How do you believe your congregation's past—the witness to Christ of its founding and now-dead heroes—informs its current ministry and mission?

Scripture for Meditation and Study...

Daniel 7:1-3, 15-18; Psalm 24; Matthew 8:5-13; Hebrews 11:29-12:2

Twelve

The Forgiveness Of Sins

On October 2, 2006, people came home from work and school and turned on the evening news to learn the horror wrecked upon the Lancaster County Amish community of Nickel Mines. A troubled truck driver named Charlie Roberts had barricaded himself inside the Amish schoolhouse at Nickel Mines and methodically shot ten girls between the ages six and thirteen. Five of the girls died, three at the scene. Charlie Roberts then shot and killed himself before police could enter the school.

The news of the shootings was shocking and sickening. But for many, it was the reaction of the families of the victims and the Amish community generally that proved most bewildering and perplexing. If there were anguished cries of why, no one heard them. No scorn was heaped upon the head of the shooter, no one called him deranged or a monster. No one from the Amish community demanded stricter gun laws or accountability from someone so that there might be "closure" for the victims, as if retribution brings healing. Instead, what was seen and heard were words and actions of forgiveness toward the shooter and reconciliation with the shooter's family.

"We must not think evil of this man," said the grandfather of one of the slain girls. Hours after the shooting, Amish neighbors came to the Roberts home to console his widow and children. Many from the Amish community attended the funeral for Roberts. Rather than labeling Roberts and avoiding his family, they, too, were treated as victims of "The Happening," as the Nickel Mines Amish community has come to refer to the shooting. As a spokesperson for the Amish families stated in the aftermath of the tragedy, "I do not think there's anybody here that wants to do anything but forgive."

Many were perplexed and bewildered by the Amish response

because they could not imagine a culture that does not support the idea of "an eye for an eye," or what the theologian Walter Wink has called "the myth of redemptive violence." The redemptive violence myth, says Wink, is the belief that violence is a necessary and appropriate response to such acts as murder and terrorism. This myth of redemptive violence promotes the belief that retributive violence is healing for the victim or victims, especially when administered by the state on the victims' behalf.

The Amish at Nickel Mines reject the myth of redemptive violence, I believe, because Jesus rejected the myth of redemptive violence. Accused of crimes against the law of his people and against the Roman authority, Jesus was unjustly condemned by an improperly convened court and crucified. When one of his disciples made a feeble attempt to violently prevent his arrest, Jesus rebuked the sword-bearer. As he hung between heaven and earth with nails through hands and feet, he did not hurl imprecations at his executioners, but rather prayed that in their ignorance they might be forgiven.

I believe in the forgiveness of sins. That's what we profess as Christians through the Apostles' Creed, but in practice we find such belief impractical and perhaps impossible. I believe in the forgiveness of sins — but only categorically. My venial sins are pardonable, but folks who did really ugly ones like rape, murder, child molestation, and the like need to burn in hell. I believe in the forgiveness of sins — but only in a theoretical kind of way. I've gotten over it, but I don't speak to my cheating ex-spouse or my abusive father. I believe in the forgiveness of sins — but only conditionally. The transgressor had better be repentant, demonstrate some contrition before the court, and make appropriate restitution.

This professed-but-unpracticed forgiveness diminishes the victims and prevents spiritual and psychological healing for them. Closure through retribution is a false myth. Exercising forgiveness unreservedly, practically, and unconditionally is the only way to healing when we have been wounded.

Making the case that certain sins can only deserve condemnation, damnation, and punishment flies in the face of the Christian profession that Christ came to redeem sinners. It is contrary to the gospel. "People will be forgiven for every sin and blasphemy," said Jesus. His only exception being a sin against the Holy Spirit — the nature of which Christianity has been discussing and arguing about for 2,000 years.

We are all sinners in need of redemption and there is no person whose sins are greater than Christ's power to redeem. I can easily identify the two greatest pastoral challenges I have faced in ministry. The first has been those few persons I have encountered who have had the spiritual hubris to believe their sins are so bad as to make them unpardonable. I can only challenge them with the example of Saul, who as a zealous Pharisee arrested Christians as heretics and sent no few of them off to prison, and perhaps torture and even death. This is the man Christ redeemed and made Paul: apostle to the nations.

The second great pastoral challenge has been those persons who know they have cheated, lied, deceived, and been unfaithful, but justify themselves as being "not as bad as so-and-so." They absurdly consider themselves what I call "meritoriously forgivable." This is the unfaithful husband who believes his indiscretions should be tolerated because he is a good material provider. This is the employee whose pilfering from the company should be overlooked because of the long hours she puts in. This is the abusive church member whose emotional scarring of others should be accepted because he or she is a faithful supporter of mission work. However, the truth is we all stand in need of forgiveness — and none of us stands beyond it.

In recent years, I have heard the phrase, "I've forgiven the person, but I'm never going to forget what they did!" Such forgiveness is a sort of mental exercise that does not make possible the reconciliation and restoration that are concurrent to real forgiveness. We certainly need to learn how our past interactions with another may have enabled behaviors that helped to create a situation or scenario in which we were victimized. Some people we encounter have psychological deformities that make certain levels of relationship with them unadvisable. But on the whole, claiming to forgive the other while turning away from him is hypocrisy.

It is notable that the Amish of Nickel Mines consoled the widowed wife and family of Charlie Roberts. They attended the funeral for Roberts. They forgave and they worked to reconcile. They remained in relationship with Roberts and his family as much as it was in their power to do so. Their forgiveness was not just theoretical. It was practical and verifiable in their move toward the one who had sinned, rather than away from him.

The Forgiveness Of Sins

"I believe in the forgiveness of sins--providing the sinner is repentant, contrite and makes restitution." When we try to practice this kind of conditional forgiveness we surrender our power to forgive and thus surrender the healing that forgiving another brings to our wound. We place it in the hands of the one who wounded us to begin with. This notion of conditional forgiveness finds its genesis in a distorted understanding of the forgiveness we are offered in Christ.

It is true that if we are to know forgiveness and reconciliation with God we must repent and turn back toward God in contrition and appropriate what God makes possible for us in Christ. But our action, or lack thereof, in response to God's forgiveness does not change God's stance toward us. Christ's redemptive death is not somehow withdrawn. God remains forgiving and wants to receive us back in love whether or not we are responsive to God's grace. One action, which remains constant, is God's. The other side of the equation — the reception of God's forgiveness — is our action to complete.

Our forgiveness of someone who has wronged us cannot be conditional upon their contrition, their apology, or their desire to make things right. Whether or not they accept the forgiveness we offer must be up to them; that we forgive without reserve is up to us. Our stance in forgiving must not change. It is only in practicing unconditionally our belief in the forgiveness of sins that we can realize the healing that brings wholeness and holiness to our lives.

The great tragedy of the happening at Nickel Mines may not be the deaths of five little girls and the trauma experienced by five others. It is perhaps the tragedy of Charlie Roberts. The notes left by this man to his family on that fateful morning revealed how deeply troubled and guilt-ridden he was. He could not forgive himself for past wrongs, which may have been real or may only have been imagined. A phone call to his wife while he was barricaded in the schoolhouse also revealed that he was angry at God, and could not forgive life for the death of his own premature daughter nine years earlier. The tragedy of Nickel Mines is the death caused by Charlie Roberts' inability to accept forgiveness and to forgive.

Sometimes life happens, and it happens badly. We operate according to ideals that are admirable, honorable and true, and in return we are dealt loss, grief and pain. The worst is that in such circumstances there is no one to blame and no one to forgive except life and ourselves. But when we see that in the middle of human history there is planted the cross, upon which the author of life and mercy surrendered himself, life is still forgivable. With Christ, life in all of its agony is still livable. I believe in the forgiveness of sins.

For Further Reflection

1. Do you believe restitution by a wrong-doer is necessary before the wrong-doer can be forgiven? If the wrong-doer is unable or unwilling to make that restitution, what then?

2. Do you believe judicial retribution (conviction and punitive sentencing of a wrong-doer) helps a victim or victims of a crime to heal? How?

3. What is the difference between forgiveness and reconciliation? Can forgiveness happen without reconciliation?

4. What new understanding about forgiveness did Jesus bring to light in his teaching? Why do you think he focused so much energy upon our need to practice forgiveness?

5. How do you understand that phrase in the Lord's Prayer, "forgive us our sins, as we forgive those who sin against us?" Does this make God's forgiveness conditional upon our willingness to forgive, or could it be the other way around?

Scripture for Meditation and Study...

Genesis 50:15-21; Psalm 32:1-5; Mark 11:20-25;

Colossians 3:12-17

Thirteen

Resurrection And The Life Everlasting

As I pondered this final clause of the Apostles' Creed, I realized how few times I have heard sermons, or preached them myself, on the subject of resurrection and everlasting life. I found this somewhat surprising, and self-revealing. As I thought about why I haven't had much to say concerning the resurrection of the dead, I came to understand that I have sometimes shied away from preaching on this subject because of the criticism it draws from religious agnostics and Christianity's "cultured despisers." Perhaps that is why I haven't heard other preachers venture into this theological terrain much, except for funerals.

Some have pejoratively called our hope of heaven "pie in the sky by-and-by when you die." Some have come to believe that life after death is a given, and that religious belief has little to do with it. Among those who understand life only in terms of biological organisms, anything beyond death is completely illogical.

In college, a group of us used to hang out at the student lounge in the main academic building. One member of the group was a young mathematics major, who quizzed me often about my faith. He frequently did so with genuine interest, but sometimes his queries were pointed and tinged with antagonism, albeit in a friendly sort of way.

"How can Christians believe in heaven or life after death or resurrection? What proof do you have? What a bizarre concept!" he would sound off. My retort always brought a smile to his face.

"So my belief in resurrection is bizarre?" I would begin. "You believe in negative numbers, right? You believe in something less than nothing? Now that's a bizarre concept! I believe that beyond death there is something other than nothing." Yet I had to own that I had no empirical evidence to prove that the dead are raised and that there is life beyond our experience of dying.

Reconsidering the Apostle's Creed

At the time I write this, the cover of a recent edition of *Newsweek* magazine features outstretched hands reaching upward toward a sunlit sky. Superimposed over the image is the title for the cover story: "Heaven Is Real: A Doctor's Experience of the Afterlife." In the article, Dr. Eben Alexander told the story of his near-death experience while in a seven-day coma resulting from bacterial meningitis. Dr. Alexander, a neuroscientist, wrote:

> In the fall of 2008... after seven days in a coma during which the human part of my brain, the neocortex, was inactivated, I experienced something so profound that it gave me a scientific reason to believe in consciousness after death.[10]

He explained that neuroscience maintains that the cortex of the brain produces thought, emotion, and all that makes us human. However, his experience of life outside of his brain and body occurred while his neocortex was completely inactive according to all scientific measure. Dr. Alexander continued in the course of the article writing about seeing spiritual beings, having overwhelming feelings of being loved, and encountering the divine as a brilliantly bright yet deep darkness. Like Saint John the Divine, who wrote in Revelation of one seated on a throne who "looks like jasper and carnelian" surrounded by a "rainbow that looks like an emerald" (Revelation 4:3), there are times when Dr. Alexander's experience challenges his ability to describe it. For him, this experience was proof of an afterlife. His story is riveting. For many of us, it may be a source of some comfort. Yet, for all of that, this account of near-death experience, like so many others, does not prove resurrection and life everlasting any more than my rebuttal to my college friend many years ago.

If we cannot prove, scientifically, that the dead are raised and that there is life everlasting after we die, what can we say faithfully in support of our Christian profession of faith?

We can say we believe that those who die in Christ shall be raised because of Christ's own actions and words that we find in the New Testament. In the upper room, prior to his arrest,

---

10 *Newsweek*, October 15, 2012.

Resurrection And The Life Everlasting

he reassured his distraught disciples by telling them, "In my Father's house there are many dwelling places. If it were not so, would I have told you that I go to prepare a place for you? And if I go and prepare a place for you, I will come again and take you to myself, so that where I am, you may be also" (John 14:2-3). To a condemned thief dying next to him on a cross, he promised, "Truly I tell you, today you will be with me in paradise" (Luke 23:43). As he himself died, he cried out, "Father, into your hands I commend my spirit" (Luke 23:46). These words tell us that the one we profess as Lord and Savior was confident that abundant life in the immediate presence of God lay beyond the agony of dying.

Furthermore, we may continue to point to the New Testament witness, particularly that of Saint Paul. In writing to the Corinthians, some of whom questioned the veracity of the resurrection of the dead, the apostle wrote that the resurrection of Jesus, while unique in itself, was a pattern for those who have faith in him. "Now if Christ is proclaimed as raised from the dead," writes Paul, "how can some of you say there is no resurrection of the dead?... But in fact Christ has been raised from the dead, the firstfruits of those who have died" (1 Corinthians 15:12, 20). In sharing his faith by letter with Christians at Rome, Paul wrote, "If the Spirit of him who raised Jesus from the dead dwells in you, he who raised Christ from the dead will give life to your mortal bodies also through his Spirit that dwells in you" (Romans 8:11). And the author of the letter to the Hebrews writes, with great emotion, of the widows of faithful martyrs, who received their dead by resurrection, of those who faced torture in order to know a better resurrection, and of a great cloud of witnesses who have died and yet are alive (Hebrews 11:35, 12:1).

Why should we point to these ancient words as the basis for our belief about resurrection and life everlasting, rather than the more contemporary witness to life beyond dying that we get from firsthand stories of near death experiences? Because accounts of near death experience are about personal survival of individual consciousness after death — that's not Christian resurrection and life everlasting.

Our profession of belief in resurrection is about the transcendence of death in, and because of, relationship--our relationship with the resurrected Jesus Christ and the community that is his body. Read the New Testament accounts closely. Jesus talked about rooms in the Father's house, about being with him and about being with his heavenly Father. Paul wrote of everlasting life as the consequence of being indwelt by the Spirit of God. The author of Hebrews, after recounting the heroes of the faith who died in hope of resurrection, wrote, "Yet all these, though they were commended for their faith, did not receive what was promised, since God had provided something better so that they would not, apart from us, be made perfect" (Hebrews 11:39-40).

Christian belief in resurrection and life everlasting is not based upon an idea that we are created with an ethereal and immortal soul. It is not about human consciousness that at times defies the boundaries of modern science. It is not about the latest revelations concerning life and our universe that come via quantum physics. Resurrection and life everlasting is not about me or you as individuals. It is about relationship. It's about God and it's about us and God. It is based upon love and relationship and community in Jesus Christ.

Dying is not an ending, or a new beginning, but a translation and transformation into a fuller way of being in relationship with God. We are raised to life in God because in relationship with Jesus Christ we share in life that cannot be snuffed by death. Because we are in relationship with Jesus, and have faith in him, we live in and with the very power of life itself. We experience that relationship of love and everlasting life now personally and individually, but we are held in it through life and through dying because of our place in that community we call the church — the body of Christ.

I have not preached often across the course of my ministry on resurrection and life everlasting. I have perhaps heard too loudly the protests of the scoffers — and they have not all been outside of the church. In one congregation where I was pastor, I had a sparring partner similar to my math major college friend. This woman made it clear that she admired the moral life and teaching of Jesus, but she found belief in his healings, the resurrection, and life everlasting so much hogwash. "When you're dead, you're dead," she would say, "that's all there is to it."

One Easter Sunday, after preaching the resurrection of Christ,

Resurrection And The Life Everlasting

I was confronted by this church member. "That sermon was full of holes!" she said to me. "You didn't say anything to prove the resurrection happened! How could you do this? You asked all these people to take what you say as true simply on faith!"

I looked at her for a moment, angry at first, but then my reaction softened. I felt a little sad, and I said to her, "That's right. I did ask all these people to take the truth of Jesus' resurrection, and ours, purely on faith. But let's be clear about one thing," I continued. "I did not ask them to accept it on faith in what I say, but I asked them to accept it as true because of their faith in Jesus Christ."

Death does not have the final say, not because we believe in a catalog of propositional statements we call a creed. But our creed points to one in whom death is transcended, in whom we do have faith, in whom we place our total trust. Our creed points to one who loves us even unto and beyond death. I believe in the resurrection of the dead and the life everlasting, because I believe in Jesus Christ.

For Further Reflection

1. What would you tell someone of another faith about Christian belief in eternal life beyond death?

2. How do you see Dr. Alexander's testimony in light of Christian belief in resurrection? Are the two compatible? How are they different?

3. How do you respond to the idea that it is relationship with God in Jesus Christ that is the only foundation for our belief in life everlasting? Does this necessarily deny the validity of claims to immortality made by other faiths?

4. Do you know Christians who do not believe, or remain agnostic, about life everlasting? What do you think prevents them from professing faith in resurrection?

5. Is the transformation of your relationship with God into one of eternal intimacy your primary hope for everlasting life? If not, what is?

Scripture for Meditation and Study:

Daniel 12:1-13; Psalm 30; John 20:26-29;
1 Corinthians 15

www.ingramcontent.com/pod-product-compliance
Lightning Source LLC
Chambersburg PA
CBHW051701040426
42446CB00009B/1239